GENDER ISSUES IN THE WORKPLACE

A Guide for
Physician Executives

GENDER ISSUES IN THE WORKPLACE

A Guide for
Physician Executives

Edited by J. Sim Tan, MD, FACPE

American College of Physician Executives

Two Urban Centre
Suite 200
4890 West Kennedy Boulevard
Tampa, Florida 33609
813/287-2000

ISBN: 0-924674-09-1

Library of Congress Card Number: 91-72113

Printed in the United States of America by Lithocolor, Tampa, Florida.

FOREWORD

The history of medicine includes many outstanding women physicians. In my own field of cardiology, the names of Helen Tausig, Mary Ellen Engle, and the newly nominated Director of the National Institutes of Health, Bernadine Healy, come to mind. However, it was not until the 1970s that medical school classes began to include increasing numbers of women. Over a 10-year period, representation of women in medical school classes reached its current level of 35-40 percent.

With a lag period that corresponds to the need for lengthy postgraduate training, the number of women joining medical school faculties also began to rise. Indeed, over the past decade, the proportion of women pursuing academic careers has been significantly higher than the proportion of men pursuing such careers. Our own data and those of the Association of American Medical Colleges indicate that women disproportionately filled nontenure track positions. For a given cohort of men and women joining faculties, the proportions reaching the level of associate professor was comparable, but the proportion of professors was significantly lower for women than for men. It remains unclear whether this is a discrepancy that will be improved with time or whether there are more systematic obstacles for women in promotion to professorship. The number of women who chair academic departments and serve as deans remains very low. Ironically, as of this writing, two of the three women medical school deans cited in Dr. Kanning's chapter on careers of women physicians are no longer deans. One became a university president and the second moved to a position in government.

For academic medicine, the 1990s represent some real opportunities and challenges for addressing the role of women physicians. For demographic reasons, there will be a substantial number of retirements of men from tenure track positions. The argument from the 1970s and '80s that relatively few tenure track positions were available will become much less defensible. As an increasing number of women reach tenure in professorial levels, there will be opportunities to appoint women to leadership roles. For these events to occur, it will require active efforts by academic institutions, their faculties, and administrators.

While there are many approaches that can be taken, it might be of interest to report on some of the efforts taken by one school of medicine—UCLA—to address these issues in a more systematic way. Since 1987, every search committee for a tenure track position or administrator must include at least one woman. This is the case even if there is not a woman with scientific or clinical expertise in the field for which the recruitment is taking place. This requirement serves several purposes. First, it provides women with an opportunity to participate in and learn about networking, organization, and academic politics. Women on search committees are encouraged to contact colleagues, both male and female, at other institutions in order to generate candidates for the positions. In this way, the pool of potential women candidates for each position may be increased. When the search committee considers the candidates, the consideration of women candidates is undertaken much more seriously if it occurs in the presence or under the scrutiny of a woman colleague. Clearly, all of the members of the search committee are responsible for maximizing the identification of both women and minority candidates, but the addition of a woman by policy has beneficial effects. Fortunately, there are enough women faculty to meet this requirement without an onerous burden on individuals. This is not always the case for other underrepresented minorities.

At UCLA, we encouraged the establishment of a women faculty organization. In addition to improving networking among current members of the faculty, this group is in a position to participate in recruiting women faculty and in mentoring younger women. It also is important in advancing policy issues and programs that are of interest and importance to women faculty. As a result of discussion with representatives of this group, we instituted two other important policies. First, at the time of salary negotiations, the School of Medicine Fiscal Officer generates a computer listing of the median, mean, and ranges of salaries for all faculty at each rank and step. The computer charts then show the salary for each woman at that rank and step. At the time of salary negotiations, any systematic appearance of lower salaries for women in a particular department are challenged, as are any disproportionally lower salaries for individuals. We insist on equivalent salaries for men and women with comparable training as well as with comparable responsibilities. Departments are not allowed to offer lower salaries to a woman simply because she is obligated to work locally as a consequence of the husband's situation. This was often a systematic source of lower salaries for women who do not have the degrees of freedom that their spouses might have in seeking an appointment. While we do not reveal individual salaries of any faculty, we will provide data on means, medians, and ranges at every rank and step to any faculty member who wishes to compare his or her salary against those of peers.

This is not to say that salaries are not influenced by the ability of a faculty member to generate grants or practice income, or that certain highly compensated skills do not demand higher salaries. However, gender cannot be a justification for any of these differences.

As a consequence of discussion about achieving strong academic records, the University of California adopted a plan whereby the principal child-rearing parent is allowed an additional year before required consideration of tenure. This provides more flexibility for all faculty, but particularly for women who wish to take off during and around pregnancy.

We believe that it is important to highlight success stories. We regularly feature the woman chair of one of our basic science departments who is a member of the National Academy of Sciences, not only because of her outstanding achievements but because she does represent a critically important role model for young women among our students and faculty. We have increased the number of women associate and assistant deans as well. It is important that this be understood as not a condescending action of a male-dominated environment. The women whom we recognize are outstanding and deserving of the recognition and advancement they receive. At the same time, however, I believe that it is an institutional responsibility to highlight their achievements as role models.

A sense of institutional commitment to the role of women in science and medicine is one of the most important responsibilities of academic leadership. When we highlight the necessity for an increasing proportion of women among graduate students, we will eventually form a pool for faculty appointments in basic science departments. There has been a clear increase in the proportion of women recruited and appointed to these positions. Equally important, the insidious and invidious nature of sexual harassment must be addressed in an institutional way. Although there are national data with regard to this issue, completion of anonymous surveys in our own institution served to galvanize interest and commitment by identifying that the problem was as prevalent locally as it is nationally. Moreover, the identification of mechanisms by which women could obtain confidential counseling as to how to deal with harassment without fear of retaliation has been critical.

Women are showing an increasing interest in areas of medicine that had previously not attracted them. While serving as attending physician on a general medical service recently, I had the opportunity to participate in the care of a particularly difficult patient with one of the few full-time women general surgeons on our faculty. I was particularly delighted two weeks later to see her receive one of the highly regarded outstanding clinical teaching awards from the graduating medical school class. The recognition that she received from the students not only serves to reinforce her own career but also to identify for all of the students that no area of medicine would not benefit from participation and leadership from women physicians and scientists.

There continues to be a great deal more to do. While improved housestaff hours and working conditions will improve the quality of child-rearing for both men and women, child care services continue to be inadequate and economically challenging.

As I have indicated before, the coming decade will provide some important new opportunities, as retiring faculty and administrators are replaced. The continued recognition and advancement of women in these roles will require diligence and perseverance by both men and women committed to the creation of a society in which the skills of its citizens are fully realized, regardless of gender, ethical, or racial background.

Kenneth I. Shine, MD
Dean
School of Medicine
UCLA
Los Angeles, California

April 1, 1991

PREFACE

Our Forum is a small group of men and women struggling to educate ourselves and our peers on the application of management skills in nonclinical areas. We wanted to have a program to present at the next National Conference of the College in May 1991. We also hoped that the presentation would generate more interest than the Dual Career seminar that we conducted in 1990. So, I was casting around for ways to involve our members in a worthwhile project.

The idea of producing this monograph came from one of its authors, Barbara LeTourneau, MD. After a meeting of the Forum on Women in Medicine and Management of the American College of Physician Executives about a year ago in San Antonio, she asked me if ACPE might consider publishing an article she was interested in writing on female issues in health care organizations. After a quick affirmative response, my Chair of the Forum brain took over. Why not accomplish a series of objectives at once?

At the 1990 National Institute of the College, I made my ambitious proposal to the Forum: Let's put all our collective energies together and have several authors pen articles for a monograph on gender roles. In concert with that effort, our seminar for the 1991 National Conference would have the same theme. The presentation and the monograph would give all physician executives provocative information that they could digest and discuss freely. The goal was and is to promote bilateral understanding by men and women physician executives of the similarities and differences of male-female physician leadership.

To my surprise, the group at the November meeting accepted the challenge immediately, in spite of the very short time frame in which to accomplish it all. Many volunteers offered their services to write, provide current information from their organizations, provide editing services, enlist other expert advice, speak, and so on. We quickly became a team with expertise in using Fax, Fone, and Fedex for coordination!

My heartfelt thanks go to each and every member of the Forum for their contributions and ideas. Special thanks go to Roger Schenke for his vision for the Forum, to Wes Curry for his master editing, and to both Wes and Kathleen Touchette for their cheerleading, technical assistance, and personal support. For all of us involved in this project, our goal has been sublimely simple: To promote a better understanding of the unique contributions that qualified women, given encouragement and opportunity, can make to medical management and to improvement in our health care delivery system.

J. Sim Tan, MD, FACPE
Chair
Forum on Women in Medicine and Management
American College of Physician Executives

April 1, 1991

WOMEN PHYSICIANS AS LEADERS

by J. Sim Tan, MD, FACPE

*T*he scene at the top of management is changing, as more men and women find themselves reporting to female directors. The qualities that are valued by each sex must be incorporated into the management skills of leaders of either sex. Many corporations have begun the task of training women to be able to fill more senior positions in management. It is therefore necessary to understand some common views of how subordinates rate their female supervisors. With understanding, appropriate education can lay the groundwork for success in implementing affirmative action programs for women.

FEMALE BOSSES

Management has typically been seen as a male role.[1-3] As a result, some stereotypical attitudes and behavior are exhibited by men and women alike toward female managers. Female bosses are seen as too "feminine," "too different," not really "women," or "not like us." They receive labels, such as the "pet" who attained a position by appointment by a male mentor who wants her there to do his bidding; the "mistress" who has used her femininity to achieve upward mobility; the "mother" who cares for and makes everyone feel good but will not get to the top because she is content to exercise her domestic nature; the "women's libber," the counterpart of the male chauvinist, who is forceful and goal oriented but will be rejected by her former peers when she climbs the ladder.

Studies of the characteristics of women managers have found that women in nontraditional management careers or in predominantly male fields are more likely to have had working mothers and fathers who encouraged their "masculine behavior," activities, and self-actualization concepts.[3] Korn Ferry International[4] confirmed previous studies showing a toll on family life of career women.

They surveyed 300 top women managers and found that only 49 percent were married, compared to 95 percent of male managers; 25 percent had never married; 20 percent were divorced or separated; and only one-third had children, compared to 97 percent of male managers.

A popular view exists of women in senior managerial positions as single-minded spinsters who behave as "Queen Bees"[5] and who, having sacrificed their personal lives for the organization and having attained a lofty spot, set themselves apart as unique. They also guard their positions against female colleagues aspiring to senior jobs. Some who are married feel stressed by also trying to run homes and families successfully, the "superwoman" track. The highest accolade these women receive is that they "think like men" but look feminine without being "flaky," emotional, or irresponsible.[6]

How do women attain leadership positions? Generally, the process is the same as for men, i.e., their bosses or mentors have encouraged and proposed them for their positions as they themselves move up. These promotions are more likely to occur in medium-sized organizations having mostly professional workers, where fast growth and rapid changes are being experienced. The many crises inherent under those circumstances frequently create opportunities for women to prove themselves. Other women have broken the glass-ceiling in large corporations when turmoil existed and new solutions and nontraditional ways of leading present an attractive alternative.[7] Generally, these organizations have performance standards whereby women have gained credibility by producing results. The successful women are able to maintain their "feminine" leadership style in their work environments, utilizing a more interactive approach that has been described as transactional leadership.

In a survey sponsored by the International Women's Forum, some unexpected similarities between men and women leaders were found. Men and women earned the same amount of money, and both men and women leaders paid their female subordinates about $12,000 less than a male with comparable job and skills. Additionally, as many men as women experience work-family conflicts, although the women have slightly more conflicts when children live at home.

Senior women health care administrators do not perceive themselves as less motivated, committed, or talented than their male counterparts.[8] Recent studies show that women's commitments are more likely to be tied to career opportunities and that, unless companies demonstrate affirmative action in promotions and respect for women, maternity leaves and day care programs alone will not stop their female professionals from quitting to go to other companies.[9] Many health care companies are experiencing all the undesirable effects of high turnover among female employees now.

Individual men and women will behave differently, depending on the culture and structure of their organizations rather than because of innate differences in their gender.[10] Women who use adaptive techniques to suppress negatively valued feminine traits and, instead, to copy male management attitudes may find themselves in a bind with both sexes.[11]

Women who behave autocratically may be penalized more than men who exhibit the same behaviors. In one study,[12] men and women who were deemed to be participative were rated equally favorably, but autocratic women were evaluated negatively, in contrast to autocratic men, whose evaluations, though tempered, were positive. The authors interpreted these results to mean that men have greater leeway than women to exhibit autocratic or participative leadership without suffering severe criticism from subordinates or peers. This difference may also be ascribed less to a function of sex than to the fact that women may exercise less organizational power. Women tend to judge women supervisors lower relative to men, if their competence has not been amply demonstrated, whereas men's evaluations of female supervisors are not similarly affected.[13]

What does all this mean? I think, as is confirmed in the following chapters of this book, that there is much for men and women in actual and potential positions of leadership to learn from one another. Neither the male nor the female approach to communication and management is inherently superior. They are different, and can be used effectively in different situations and for different purposes interchangeably by men and women alike. As more and more women enter the medical profession and aspire for leadership roles, they will have to clearly appreciate these gender differences. To gain maximum benefit from women in management roles, men, who currently occupy most of those roles, will have to achieve a similar appreciation and understanding.

J. Sim Tan, MD, FACPE, is Medical Director, Travelers Health Network, San Diego, Calif. She is Chairman of the Forum on Women in Medicine and Management of the American College of Physician Executives.

References

1. Basil, D. *Women in Management*. New York, N.Y.: McGraw-Hill, 1973.

2. Shepard, H. "Men in Organizations: Some Reflections." In: Sargent, A. (Ed.) *Beyond Sex Roles*. New York, N.Y.: New York West, 1977.

3. Hennig, M., and Jardim, A. *The Managerial Woman*. Garden City, N.Y.: Doubleday, Anchor Books, 1977.

4. Korn-Ferry and Association of University Programs in Health Administration. *Health Administration Employment: A Survey of Early Career Opportunities.* New York, N.Y.: Korn-Ferry International, 1987.

5. Staines, G., and others. "The Queen Bee Syndrome." *Psychology Today,* Jan. 1974.

6. Pogrebin, L. *Getting Yours: How to Make the System Work for the Working Woman.* New York, N.Y.: Avon Books, 1976.

7. Rosener, J. "Ways Women Lead." *Harvard Business Review* 68(6):119-25, Nov.-Dec. 1990.

8. Haddock, C., and Aries, N. "Career Development of Women in Health Care Administration." *Health Care Management Review* 14(3):33-40, Summer 1989.

9. Trost, C. "Women Managers Quit Not for Family but to Advance Their Corporate Climb." *Wall Street Journal,* May 2, 1990.

10. Kanter, R. "Men and Women of the Corporation Revised." *Management Review,* March 1987, pp. 14-16.

11. Haccoun, D., and others. "Sex Differences in tha Appropriateness of Supervisory Style: A Nonmanagement View." *Journal of Applied Psychology* 63(1):124-7, Feb. 1978.

12. Jago, A., and Vroom, V. "Sex Differences in the Incidence and Evaluation of Participative Leader Behaviour." *Journal of Applied Psychology* 67(6):776-83, Dec. 1982.

13. Lisenmeier, J., and Wortman, C. "Attitudes Towards Workers and Towards Their Work: More Evidence That Sex Makes a Difference." *Journal of Applied Social Psychology* 9(4):326-34, July-Aug. 1979.

CONTENTS

FOREWORD i

PREFACE v

INTRODUCTION vii

CHAPTER 1 1
Genetic and Environmental Contributions to Gender Differences
Marcia L. Comstock, MD

CHAPTER 2 17
Women in the Medical Profession: Demographics and Practice Patterns
Randy S. Ellis, MD, FACEP

CHAPTER 3 29
Gender Differences in Medical Practice
Linda Jean Lemay, MD

CHAPTER 4 35
Women Physicians in Career Tracks
Marianne D. Kanning, MD

CHAPTER 5 41
Why Do Women Choose the Careers They Choose
Barbara LeTourneau, MD, MBA

CHAPTER 6 49
Female Physicians and Human Resource Issues
Chris B. Emmons and Kathleen Yaremchuk, MD, MSA

CHAPTER 7 69
Women in the Work Force—Issues for Physician Executives
Rice Leach, MD, FACPE, and Patricia D. Mail, MPH, CHES

CHAPTER 8 83
Gender and Value Issues in Organizations—Creating the Environment
Susan L. Radecky, MD

EPILOGUE 99

CHAPTER 1

GENETIC AND ENVIRONMENTAL CONTRIBUTIONS TO GENDER DIFFERENCES

by Marcia L. Comstock, MD

Differences in style, attitudes, and values among individuals have many roots. Some are psychological, some social. All are clearly influenced by environment, e.g. family, culture, economics.

This chapter seeks to examine stereotypical socialization patterns of children and explore the influence this has on men and women as adults, as well as advantages and disadvantages of western socialization for individuals who choose medical practice. We will review recent studies of women physicians with regard to attitudes, values, and communication styles, as well as practice patterns, and raise some thought-provoking questions about what the "feminization" of medicine, coupled with increasingly sophisticated medical consumers, might mean to the future of health care delivery.

Joseph Spaeth, President of the University of Vienna in the early 1870s, took the opportunity during his inaugural address to voice his opinion that women were innately inferior to men by virtue of their lower brain weight, and also were superficial and incapable of serious study.[1] Although America had its first medical school in 1767, the first woman, Elizabeth Blackwell, was not admitted to Geneva Medical College until 1847. By 1893, Johns Hopkins became the first "prestigious" school to grant admission to women. Interestingly, we have later evidence of reverse discrimination, in that the Women's Medical College of Pennsylvania did not admit men until 1970![2]

Despite such inauspicious beginnings and continuing discrepancies in income, Heins' study of career and life patterns of men and women showed the significantly greater optimism felt by women about their careers and future, as well as overall satisfaction with their personal lives.[3] This might seem surprising, given the Detroit Physician Study's finding that these practicing women physicians bore the major burden of household responsibilities as well. But some data we will explore later show this finding is compatible with women's value set.[4]

What can be said about women's practices today? Many studies have shown women's predilection for primary care, especially in salaried positions. Studies have attributed women's lower salaries to the practice of less lucrative specialties, with an emphasis on personal interaction and on intellectual rather than technical skill. A report by the Center for Health Policy Research of the American Medical Association in 1984 showed that the length of a patient visit is virtually identical for men and women practitioners,[5] and a 1983 article in Research in Medical Education found that, contrary to a common belief, the number of hours per week worked was not a differentiating point between male and female physician practices.[6] The gap in earnings seems to be narrowing as, at least in terms of sheer numbers, women become a greater force in medicine.

It is well recognized that female patients, who seek care earlier and more readily than men, are the more frequent users of health services as well as more frequent consumers of prescription and nonprescription drugs and recipients of common testing procedures. Yet up until very recently, clinical researchers studying common disease entities, such as coronary artery disease, used only male subjects, apparently assuming disease processes and biologic responses are blind to sex differences. In addition, there was evidence of gender disparity in the performance of certain high-tech testing procedures, as well as in treatment of a number of conditions.[7]

Nonetheless, there are promising new trends. In contrast to older studies that suggested that most physicians, who were male, took men's complaints more seriously than women's, a report in 1986 showed no evidence of inequality of response to five common, potentially serious complaints. In both extent and content of care there was no difference. Some possible explanations include the younger age of the physicians and older age of the patients, as well as the fact that men and women practiced together in partnerships, possibly resulting in less sexism.[8] Further good news, as recently reported in *American Medical News*, is that the AMA House of Delegates has adopted a report, compiled by the Council on Ethical and Judicial Affairs, recommending increased involvement of women in clinical investigations, as well as studies on health issues exclusive to women. Were women to gain universal leadership visibility, the report postulates, consciousness and attention to these issues would rise.[9]

With the increase in the numbers of women on both sides of the health equation, one would assume ever-increasing feminine power and influence. For some, this change is highly welcome—those who believe it will lead to more humane, less "instrumental" care. Women, focusing as they do on "affiliation and intimacy," are felt to be more person- and less technology-oriented. Others, however, are concerned that if our society remains "sexist" (rather than becoming more androgynous), medicine will be lowered in status and financial rewards and will assume attributes typical of other "feminine" occupations[10] where "females are used, abused, and underpaid."[11]

Clearly, then, a move toward a more middle ground, with less sexism on both sides, should be to everyone's advantage. In order to ensure more rather than less benefit to society in general from the influx of women, several important variables must be influenced. Many factors exist that tend to keep women in positions of less power that are not related to family issues or practice patterns, but are more the offshoot of socialization and communication styles.

Mary E. Costanza, MD, points out that hospitals almost always follow a male-oriented (i.e., akin to military or sports) model that advocates conquering an opponent in the success/achievement game. This game, she feels, is antithetical to female values of caring for and working with others, that is, helping all to succeed. Carol Gilligan, Professor of Education at Harvard, believes there are differences in normative thinking that can be categorized as typically male (abstract, hierarchical) or female (specific, interrelated, inclusive) values.[12] Costanza goes on to say, "The possibility of female-identified leadership emerging from a male dominant system...seems remote."[13]

So, given that there is likely to be at least some truth to the notion that women still face significant struggles in medicine as elsewhere in life competition, what are some of the patterns of socialization in our society that contribute to conflicts between men and women?

In her recently published book *You Just Don't Understand*, sociolinguist Deborah Tannen explores these issues in depth. One assumption, fundamental to her research, is that all humans need both intimacy and independence, but whereas women focus on the former, men focus on the latter. For men, life is a hierarchical social order in which one is either one-up or one-down. In conversation, the purpose is negotiation in an attempt to gain that upper hand and in so doing preserve independence. Power comes from individuals' acting in opposition to one another. Life is a contest in which one is repeatedly challenged and must perform to avoid risk of failure. On the other hand, women approach life as a series of connections, and in conversations the purpose is negotiation for closeness, that is, to seek and give support and reach agreements. The source of power is community, and the life struggle is against the danger of being cut off.[14] Women, of course, also want status, but it is pursued in the guise of connection.

Men certainly also want involvement, but it tends to be pursued in the guise of opposition.[15]

Tannen submits that, from early childhood, men and women speak and hear a different language. Although results of studies are conflicting when it comes to establishing which of the sexes talks more, Tannen feels the answer depends on whether you consider the private or public arena. For women, the language of conversation is primarily "rapport."[16] Therefore, in small groups of intimates or one-on-one with someone well known, women are comfortable interacting fully. Men, on the other hand, learn from childhood to use talking to get and keep attention, so they are more comfortable than women in talking with groups, particularly if the group is not well known. Therefore, their skill at "verbal performance" or "report-talk" may well give them an advantage in public meetings and contribute to a negative perception of women's leadership ability. Women have been shown to feel a situation is more "public" if men are present. Their orientation to language results in the use of more personal experience and anecdotal evidence, rather than abstract argumentation, to make a point. This type of evidence may not carry much weight with men. Much evidence also exists to support the notion that men's styles in general are evaluated more positively and are taken as the norm. Male-female conversations are more like men's, that is, resemble "report-talk." Thus women must make more adjustments and are at a disadvantage because of less experience conducting conversation in this way. Therefore, being in a mixed, rather than same sex, meeting makes more difference to women than to men.[17] Although men who do all the talking at meetings may be seen as "dominating," the metamessage may be one of equality, that is, "we are all equals...competing for the floor." But, as Tannen points out, "...being admitted as an equal is not in itself assurance of equal opportunity, if one is not accustomed to playing the game the way it is being played."[18]

Another disadvantage women suffer in attempting to achieve positions of power relates to a tendency to be more modest and self-effacing. This, too, has its roots in childhood. Boys' access to success is through achievements and skill (e.g., sports), and they define themselves in these terms. Early on, they learn to get what they want (i.e., status) by displaying authority. Girls succeed in connections to people and define themselves in terms of overall character.[19] They feel it is crucial to be liked by peers, and they grow up learning that to stand out is not attractive. Girls at play are frequently heard to criticize peers who appear better or brighter. It seems it is a violation of their egalitarian ethic that stresses similarity and connection.[20]

There is substantial evidence that some resultant fear of success may carry over into adult life. This can be reinforced by the fact that traits admired in men, such as self-confident displays of expertise or accomplishments or attempts to "get the floor," if manifested by a woman result in criticism and alienation. Attempting to succeed using men's rules results in a woman's being labeled aggressive and unfeminine.[21] Whereas men who are forceful, direct, logical, and powerful have enhanced value, similar women undercut their femininity.[22]

In considering women as "managers" rather than"leaders," there are further contrasts. A negative offshoot of the female perception of the "community" as the source of power is the conviction that women should not act alone. This is a hindrance to quick decision making. By the same token, men's conviction that they must act independently has negative consequences if they don't have all the information. (Interestingly, studies of the most successful men in business and science show them to be extremely competent, though not very competitive!) On the positive side, women's inclination to seek agreement may well be an advantage in management, as people are more likely to be happy if they have a say in policy-making decisions. Women are seen as more approachable. This may relate to the assumption that their intrinsic conflict avoidance makes it less likely they will respond harshly in anger.[23]

We have seen some general ways in which stereotypical socialization childhood experiences may affect adult values and style. But an interesting question relates to women who choose a medical career. Are they very typically feminine or do they have some of the reputedly masculine qualities, such as assertiveness and competitiveness? Does medical school and postgraduate training change fundamental values and attributes?

Studies done up to the early 1970s showed personality differences on measures of affiliation, autonomy, aggression, and nurturance between male and female medical students, but the findings were not consistent. Blakeney et al. reported in 1982 on a study of the personality characteristics of women entering medical school in the '70s. They concluded that the typical student changed little over the decade, although the numbers of women increased significantly. Using the Omnibus Personality Inventory and the Minnesota Multiphasic Personality Inventory (MMPI) to assess attitudes, values, and interests, the researchers found that female students were happy, independent, socially outgoing, sensitive, concerned about others, optimistic, well adjusted, and verbal. They were nonauthoritarian but possessed a positive self-image. They had cultural as well as scientific interests and tended to be somewhat liberal and quite idealistic. They had low scores on "practical outlook." When it came to intellectual challenge, they were conservative—they were not experimental and disliked ambiguity.

These women were troubled, however, by a perceived lack of role models, as they did not wish to emulate totally career-oriented, childless, frequently single physicians of the past. They believed that at the time they entered medicine, it was necessary to be aggressive and very determined to survive. Some corroborating evidence comes from MMPI results on a small group of female medical students in 1959 and 1960. Although very similar overall to the students studied 20 years later, they saw themselves as somewhat less sensitive and more obsessive. Because of the constancy over time of female medical students' personalities, the authors postulate that if women practitioners differ significantly from ideal role models as seen by students, these differences developed after starting medical school![24] Two 1953 studies by Schofield cited in the article may offer some explanation. He found that male medical students, particularly the top students, showed "defeminization" of activities and interests by the third year.

A 1987 study attempted to investigate how gender is related to personality in medical students and to their perceptions of physicians, through the use of Personality Research Form-A (PRF-A). Both male and female students tended to perceive most physicians as similar to male, but not female, physicians. In the students themselves, no overall difference between the sexes was found on personality traits. On certain scales, they differed in similar direction from both male and female norms. That is, there was more evidence for androgynous traits. Yet the different characteristics attributed to male and female practitioners followed traditional stereotypes. Male students felt women physicians fit their stereotype of females in general—nurturant, orderly, and avoiding of harm, as well as less dominant, aggressive, autonomous, and enduring. Female students reportedly saw both sexes of physicians traditionally, but, when answering for "most physicians," they saw them as similar to female physicians for half the traits and similar to male physicians for the other half. Female physicians were rated higher than either "most" or "male" physicians on achievement, order, endurance, and understanding. This supports the female students' conviction, also noted by Blakeney, that for them success in medicine requires deviation from traditional norms. They apparently felt more organization, intellectual curiosity, determination, and persistence is needed. Because the male students saw male physicians as higher on these traits as well as on affiliation, the authors postulate that both groups recognized these industrious, yet humane, qualities as those sought by patients, and thus identify them with their own sex.

A final important finding of this study is that the women students had a greater disparity than the men between "self" versus "most physicians" for 10 of the 14 traits. These gaps represent potential areas of stress for these aspiring physicians.[25]

I would now like to turn attention from attitudes, values, and personality traits of medical students to women as health care practitioners and to their relationships with their patients as well as with significant others. As we have seen in reviewing some of Tannen's work, affiliation and relationships are a much more integral part of the fabric of a woman's life than of a man's. For this reason, any analysis of women practitioners must also address the potential role strain in attempting to achieve "status" in their careers yet maintain "intimacy" in the personal domain.

Although many authors have focused on the negative aspect of combining professional and family responsibilities, there are contradictory findings, and it sometimes seems private and professional roles enhance each another. Ducker found that, in a group of female physicians who expressed strong satisfaction with their lives in general, the personal domain was even more central to well-being; that is, satisfaction here was more correlated with overall life satisfaction. Furthermore, stronger commitment to work was associated with a drop in satisfaction with personal life because of feelings of loss of control. The key, however, seemed to be emotional support of the spouse above any other factor.[26] Perhaps this was a mitigating factor in the overall optimism found by Heins in women physicians.[27]

What of the relationship between this female physician and her patients? Is she better socialized or more ill-prepared than her male colleague for the one-on-one relationship defined by the medical encounter? It could be argued, and is by Tannen, that although boys' games better prepare them for life in the "work world" because of their complex roles and rules, girls' games, with their complexity in verbally managing interpersonal relationships, may well provide the advantage in the therapeutic arena.[28]

Prior to the advent of pharmaceuticals and technology, the only "tool" of value in the physician's armamentarium was bedside manner—the laying on of hands, the developing of rapport and affiliation and community between physician and patient. No other intervention contributed as much to final outcome. As the perceived importance and intrusive use of scientific technology escalated, it seems that a different personality type was attracted to medicine. As was already alluded to, the rigors of medical school may have served to eliminate or negatively modify interpersonal skills in the past.[29] Because there is growing appreciation for the valuable contribution made to the quality of a medical encounter by a clear metamessage of rapport and caring between doctor and patient, it would serve all physicians well to consciously strive to hone interpersonal skills.

Female physicians are said to be more sensitive to the doctor-patient relationship and more accepting of the patient's feelings. Further, they are believed to attend to the humanistic and social aspects of patient care to a greater degree than do male colleagues. Yet it seems that here, too, gender differences are declining. Although some have postulated that women are more interested in health counseling and patient education, i.e., information-giving, there is recent evidence that now differences are greater in attitude than practice.[30]

The criticality of information sharing in medical practice is supported by two observations:

- The only factor affecting medical compliance directly amenable to altera-
tion is physician input.

- There are several studies attesting to the importance placed by patients on
information flow in contributing to their sense of satisfaction.[31]

Comstock also found high correlation between patient satisfaction and common courtesy (such as formally greeting and discharging the patient) and what
was perceived as active listening (using open-ended questions, eliciting details,
and allowing the patient the opportunity to ask questions). However, physical
attention and physical appearance did not correlate with satisfaction, and length
of encounters correlated only weakly, suggesting that the quality of the interaction was more important than its length. Thus, to this group of patients, verbal
skills were much more important than nonverbal behavior. This study found no
difference in mean ratings of caring behaviors or overall patient satisfaction
between male and female physicians, but the most satisfaction was expressed by
women patients regarding women physicians.[32] Indeed, quality of communication between doctor and patient has been found to strongly influence not only
overall satisfaction, but also appointment keeping and compliance.[33]

In Tannen's book, we find further consideration of skill development by
males and females in verbal behavior. First, I will consider information giving. It
might seem, given their greater sense of comfort with asymmetrical, that is, one-
up, one-down, relationships, that men might be more adept at this verbal skill.
After all, the act of providing information, like the act of helping, giving advice,
or protecting, frames the giver in a one-up position. Tannen goes on to add that
for men a pleasant feeling of superiority due to greater command of the subject
matter is reinforced when the other person does not understand.[34] This may be
why Weisman confirmed that patients frequently experience clearer explanations from female physicians.[35] Therefore, although men may be more comfortable when giving advice or information, effective communication can be hin-
dered with a patient who is less able to grasp complex concepts or one who, like
many women, prefers a more symmetrical exchange of information. Being facile
problem solvers, as well as independent thinkers, men are also hesitant to ask for
assistance and may be reluctant to admit that they don't have the answer or that
they made a mistake, clearly a potential tragic flaw in a physician.[36]

To the extent that the above traits exist in a patient, the communication skills
of the physician can be sorely taxed by the effort required to extract pertinent
symptoms, concerns, and questions from a patient who is reluctant to ask for help
or advice or who feels that admitting to a problem puts him- or herself in a one-
down position! Personal experience for me does support, to some extent, the
contention that, when in the patient role, it is women who more freely and

articulately describe symptoms and complaints and, as shown in several studies, ask the most questions. (Perhaps this is why it seems women accompany their husbands to a medical appointment for the purpose of clarifying a situation more often than vice versa.) One positive outcome, according to Waitzkin, seems to be that women get more time and more answers! Although he did not find that men physicians withheld information and talked down to women patients, several studies report that, in general, physicians underestimate the amount of information patients desire. However, in this study social class and educational level, more than patient sex, influenced how much information was provided.[37]

In addition to information-giving, another verbal skill highly valued by patients is active listening. Just as the act of giving information frames the giver in a higher status position, the act of listening does the opposite. Several studies cited by Tannen confirm the notion that while boys are learning to gain and hold center stage by talking, girls are learning to listen.[38] As adults, women in conversations tend to ask questions, offer support, and give more "listening responses," in effect producing a running feedback loop, the purpose of which is to encourage the other person to talk and thus reinforce connection. Men's strategies are different. They tend to give few listening responses, make statements rather than ask questions, and are more likely to challenge than agree, essentially positioning themselves as incipient speakers.[39]

But do men really interrupt women more often? Tannen points out that different conversational styles are more than a matter of gender. There are cultural differences and regional differences—even differences that arise because of family patterns. She describes two main styles, "high-considerateness" and "high involvement." But one's style is not an absolute. It is contrasts in style that make the difference. Individual style is on a continuum, and a person perceived as interrupting by someone who culturally expects longer pauses is frequently of the "high-involvement" style, whether male or female. This individual may, in turn, feel the same way about someone who uses shorter pauses. As a result, cultural or style differences often result in unfair stereotypes and generalizations, such as that certain ethnic groups are pushy and men are domineering. Nonetheless, although women, who are described by Tannen as "cooperative overlappers," may interrupt and overlap in casual conversation, i.e., "rapport-talk," men are more likely to do so in more formal "report-talk" scenarios, for reasons already discussed.[40]

Carol Weisman reviewed recent literature on the matter of communication between women and their health care providers. She was specifically interested in the effect of gender (either patients' or physicians') on the process of communication and its outcome. Findings confirmed that female practitioners, like females in general, are more highly oriented toward communication issues and that they tend to value exchange of information and questioning by patients.

They also prefer patients who are assertive and good communicators. Women physicians were also found to be better at interpreting nonverbal cues, such as facial expression. Weisman postulates that a female patient, by the same token, may be adept at interpreting negative emotional cues from her physician! Weisman also found evidence in the literature to support the contention that men speak at greater length, that is, engage in "report-talk," and more typically demonstrate signs of verbal dominance, such as interrupting patients.[41] Hypothetically, according to Weisman, female physicians' enhanced effectiveness as communicators, particularly with female patients, may, in fact, contribute to better outcomes under certain circumstances.

Some authors have found that an increase in social, just as in cultural, difference impedes communication. Thus, same-sex dyads, which are more socially symmetrical, might be thought to facilitate communication. Diagnosis and treatment of medical ailments requires participation by both physician and patient in a problem-solving process. There is ample evidence that disclosure of symptoms in a timely and accurate manner is less than ideal. Young found an increased willingness to disclose symptoms or concerns of a personal or emotional nature to a physician of the same sex. However, the sex of the physician did not influence disclosure of symptoms of a general nature. This confirmed other studies that found much less reticence to disclose logical, technical, aspects of their problems than the irrational, emotionally laden components.[42] Therefore, it might be concluded that when sex-specific conditions, such as dysmenorrhea or breast cancer, or issues of a highly sensitive nature, for example, depression, sexual dysfunction, or family planning, are being discussed, female physicians may positively affect outcome for female patients. Weisman believes the same is true in treatment of chronic diseases or in life-style modification, but this is more difficult to support.[43]

Female or male dyads should certainly also be beneficial from a therapeutic perspective when a patient strongly prefers a physician of the same sex. Studies from the '70s were conflicting with regard to patients' preferences for a physician of a particular sex, but related, somewhat inconsistently, to patient age and socioeconomic status. Newer data suggest that both sexes prefer a physician of the same sex for visits requiring genital examination or discussion of personal or emotional problems.[44] Data reported in 1990 in the Journal of Family Practice corroborated again Young's findings on symptom disclosure. The study sought to determine physician sex preferences for male and female patients, establish whether or not increased experience with female physicians related to expressed preferences, and examined the issue of why preferences exist. Considerations included expectations of behavior based on sex stereotype as well as priorities regarding physician characteristics.

Of the patients surveyed in this study, about half overall (slightly more women than men) expressed a preference for sex of physician for general care. The sample had high levels of experience with female physicians, and it is postulated that experience may relate to preference. There was differential, however, with regard to the type of clinical situation presented; two-thirds of patients expressed sex preference for genital exams, about half for behavioral problems (both tending to prefer a woman), and only slightly over a quarter for general medical problems. There was also evidence to support sex stereotyping of physician behavior, with "humaneness" more typically associated with females and technical competence with males. "Hurriedness" was also associated with males, particularly by the group of patients preferring a female. The author was unclear as to whether this was due to the experience with male doctors of the patients who preferred a female physician or merely evidence of a traditional stereotype. This patient set placed the highest value on humanness and comprehensiveness; technical competence, unlike in some other studies, was not seen as a top priority.[45]

Despite all that has been written about values, habits, attitudes, and styles that are typically masculine or feminine, the truth is that gender is but one influence on character and may not be more important than culture, ethnicity, religious affiliation, environment, or personal experience. In fact, a recent *New York Times* article pointed out a cultural contrast that sounds strangely like what we have defined as gender contrast between cherished American values of self-reliance and individualism (typically believed to be masculine) and the interdependence and self-effacing modesty (typically believed to be more feminine) of non-Western cultures. It is important to realize that we all struggle in the face of pressures and influences that can become burdensome.

To quote Deborah Tannen on the disparate concerns of men and women socialized in our culture: "The pressure to maintain connections with others while appearing skillful and knowledgeable and while negotiating relative rank can become a burden for males. The pressure to achieve status while avoiding conflict and appearing no better than anyone else can become a burden for females."[46]

By understanding our habitual ways of communicating, as well as how effective or ineffective we are in different situations, we can override automatic impulses and modify our style when it fails to produce the desired result. In other words, we would all do well to increase our flexibility and have more than one strategy at our disposal. Nonetheless, I would take exception to the contention of Mary Costanza, MD, who views females as intrinsically "calmer, fairer, more apt to see all sides to the problem, more conciliatory, more collegial," and men as "too fiesty, too competitive, too short-tempered, too trigger-happy, and too aggressive to lead."[47] Rather than more clearly drawing the lines of battle, an increasing number of senior executives recognize that they must embody some of the inherent qualities of both sexes in their leadership skills.

Health care consumers today are increasingly sophisticated and knowledge-able. That they are more demanding and critical of their physicians is validated by Comstock's finding in her study on physician behaviors that patients under 40 tended to rate physicians lower. Access to medical information, as well as interest in wellness, has increased. With this new knowledge and interest comes a strong desire on the part of many patients to have a voice in their medical care. Studies have already shown that all patients value "humanness" and compre-hensiveness in care. Necessary components for humanness include courtesy, respect, and a willingness to listen and clearly respond to questions in an unhur-ried manner. As medicine becomes increasingly competitive, those practitio-ners, be they male or female, whose verbal skills are as honed as their diagnostic skills will have the competitive advantage. Significant contributions to organiza-tional success requires the integration of both male and female approaches to communication and management.

Marcia L. Comstock, MD, is Research and Development Health Services Director, A T & T Bell Laboratories, Short Hills, New Jersey.

References

1.   Heins, M. "Update: Women in Medicine." *Journal of the American Medical Women's Association* 40(2):43, March-April 1985.

2.   *Ibid.*, p. 44.

3.   *Ibid.*, p. 47.

4.   *Ibid.*, p. 48.

5.   *Ibid.*, p. 46.

6.   *Ibid.*, p. 45.

7.   Hall, J., and others. "Performance Quality, Gender, and Professional Role. A Study of Physicians and Nonphysicians in 16 Ambulatory Care Practices." *Medical Care* 28(6):489-490, June 1990.

8.   Greer, S., and others. "Responses of Male and Female Physicians to Medical Complaints in Male and Female Patients." *Journal of Family Practice.* 23(1):52, July 1986.

9.   *American Medical News*, Dec. 14, 1990.

10.   Silver, G. "The Feminization of Medical Practice." *Lancet* 335(8698):1149-50, May 12, 1990.

11. Bernstein, A. "Gender Equity." *Journal of the American Medical Women's Association* 44(3):84, May-June 1989.

12. Costanza, M. "Women in Medical Leadership." *Journal of the American Medical Women's Association* 44(6):185-6, Nov.-Dec. 1989.

13. *Ibid.*, p. 185.

14. Tannen, D. *You Just Don't Understand: Women and Men in Conversation.* New York, N.Y.: W. Morrow & Co., Inc., 1990, p. 178.

15. *Ibid.*, pp. 24-26.

16. *Ibid.*, p. 77.

17. *Ibid.*, p. 235.

18. *Ibid.*, p. 95.

19. *Ibid.*, p. 107.

20. *Ibid.*, p. 180.

21. *Ibid.*, p. 224.

22. *Ibid.*, p. 243.

23. *Ibid.*, pp. 181-4.

24. Blakeney, P., and others. "Personality Characteristics of Women Entering Medical School Over a 10-Year Period." *Journal of Medical Education* 57(1):44-7, Jan. 1982.

25. Dralle, D., and others. "Sex Role Stereotypes in Freshman Medical Students' Perceptions of Self and Physicians." *Journal of the American Medical Women's Association* 42(3):78-80, May-June 1987.

26. Ducker, D. "Life Satisfactions for Women Physicians." *Journal of the American Medical Women's Association* 42(2):58, March-April 1987.

27. Heins, *op. cit*, p. 47.

28. Tannen, *op. cit*, p. 181.

29. Comstock, L., and others. "Physician Behaviors that Correlate with Patient Satisfaction." *Journal of Medical Education* 57(2):105, Feb. 1982.

30. Maheux, B., and others. "Female Medical Practitioners. More Preventive and Patient Oriented?" *Medical Care* 28(1):90-1, Jan. 1990.

31. Comstock, *op. cit*, p. 112.

32. Comstock, *op. cit*, p. 109.

33. Weisman, C. "Communication between Women and Their Health Care Providers: Research Findings and Unanswered Questions." *Public Health Reports*, Suppl., July-Aug. 1987, p. 148.

34. Tannen, *op. cit*, p. 68.

35. Weisman, *op. cit*, p. 147.

36. Tannen, *op. cit*, p. 64.

37. Weisman, *op. cit*, p. 149.

38. Tannen, *op. cit*, pp. 138-9.

39. *Ibid.*, p. 142.

40. *Ibid.*, p. 121.

41. Weisman, *op. cit*, p. 149.

42. Young, J. "Symptom Disclosure to Male and Female Physicians: Effects of Sex, Physical Attractiveness, and Symptom Type." *Journal of Behavioral Medicine* 2(2):166-7, June 1979.

43. Weisman, *op. cit*, p. 150.

44. Fennema, K., and others. "Sex of Physician: Patients' Preferences and Stereotypes." *Journal of Family Practice* 30(4):443-4, April 1990.

45. *Ibid.*, pp. 445-6.

46. *Ibid.*, p. 293.

47. Costanza, *op. cit*, p. 186.

Further Readings

Dickstein, L. "Female Physicians in the 1980s: Personal and Family Attitudes and Values." *Journal of the American Medical Women's Association* 45(4):122-6, July-Aug. 1990.

Dole, L. "The Struggle for Balance." *California Physician* 7(11):36-41, Nov. 1990.

Gilligan, C. *In a Different Voice*. Cambridge, Mass.: Harvard University Press, 1982.

Lorber, J. "More Women Physicians: Will it Mean More Humane Health Care?" *Social Policy* 16(1):50-4, Summer 1985.

Morantz-Sanchez, R. "Not Feminized but Humanized." *New Jersey Medicine* 85(5):363-70, May 1988.

Shore, E. "Making a Difference in Academia." *Journal of the American Medical Women's Association* 39(3):81-3,106, May-June 1984.

CHAPTER 2

WOMEN IN THE MEDICAL PROFESSION: DEMOGRAPHICS AND PRACTICE PATTERNS

by Randy S. Ellis, MD, FACEP

*M*anagers in the health care industry have been faced with momentous changes over the past two decades. One of the most important has been a change in their own ranks: today, more than half the graduates of master's degree programs in health administration are women.[1] Technological advances have changed the products offered and the capital outlay and financing required. These changed products are being offered to an altered consumer population. More than half of the patients in acute care hospitals are women, as are 80 percent of nursing home patients and 90 percent of nursing home patients over the age of 85. Of the 25 most commonly performed operative procedures, 11 are done exclusively on women.[1]

This feminization of the industry is continued into the labor force. Of nurses, 96 percent are women, as are 80 percent of the overall health care work force.

In addition, the past two decades have seen a marked increase in the number of women physicians actively practicing medicine. Between 1970 and 1985, while the total number of practicing physicians grew by 66 percent, the number of women physicians increased by more than three times that amount. The number of active women physicians will expand from about 55,000 in 1981 to more than 141,000 by the year 2000, an increase of 153 percent.[2] Because the total number of active physicians is expected to increase during this same period by

FIGURE 1:

Number of Male and Female Medical School Applicants for Selected Years,
1973-89 *(Source: Association of American Medical Colleges: AMA Women in Medicine Study)*

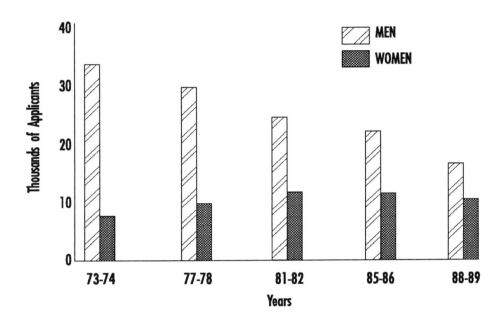

only 27 percent, the proportion of female physicians will increase from 12 to 20 percent of all physicians.[2] Today, 37 percent of first-year medical students are women, as are 15 percent of active physicians; it is estimated that, by 2010, 29 percent of active physicians will be women. For every 8 college women who want to be nurses, 10 want to be physicians.[1]

Because of some unique characteristics of women physicians, this feminization of the medical profession will have important ramifications on the delivery of health care in the coming decades.

WOMEN MEDICAL STUDENTS

Women are entering medical schools and training programs in unprecedented numbers. The percentage of women college graduates applying to medical school has tripled since 1970, going from 0.8 percent to the current rate of 2.3 percent. At the same time, there has been a drop from 4.9 percent to 4.2 percent in the percentage of male college graduates applying to medical school.[3]

When the absolute numbers of applicants are considered (see figure 1, page 18), the dramatic decrease in the number of male applicants (more than 50 percent) between the years 1973-74 and 1988-89 is immediately noticed.

The increased number of women applicants to medical schools has been the result of three main factors. The enactment of federal antidiscrimination legislation and the adoption of the equal opportunity resolution by the Association of American Medical Colleges in 1970 removed the bureaucratic barriers to women's entrance into the medical profession. However, the emerging feminist movement, which helped women to recognize their potential and to improve their aspirations and encouraged them to seek nontraditional roles, was the most important factor.[4]

While the increased number of women applying and being accepted to medical school is easily explained, the decreasing number of male applicants is not. Traditionally, medicine has been at the top of the list of prestigious professions. Previously male-dominated and well-paid, it ranked number one in public respect. However, in countries where the profession is considerably less well-paid and prestigious, most of the doctors are women.[5] The recent decline of the profession's standing, both in public opinion and as far as economic remuneration is concerned, may well be turning male applicants from the profession.

WOMEN IN ACADEMIA

Women have always been involved in medical education. In fact, since at least the 1950s, a greater proportion of graduating women than men found jobs on medical school faculties.[4] However, when distribution among faculty ranks and tenures is considered, some distressing trends emerge. In 1981, women faculty were concentrated in the lower ranks, with greater than two-thirds in the assistant professor and instructor categories (see figure 2, page 20). While this may be a result of the shorter length of time that women have been "protected" by the nondiscrimination legislation, a review of the data from 1988 shows a similar pattern. In fact, in the intervening 7 years, there has actually been a decrease in the number of women at the professor level.

The reasons behind this skewed distribution have been disclosed by numerous studies. Female faculty are found in the higher ranks less frequently than male faculty, and the disparity increases with age. In a 1982 study of women aged 47 or greater, only 28 percent had attained the rank of full professor, compared with 61 percent of the men in the same age group.[6] Male and female faculty members are not promoted from the rank of assistant professor at the same rate—the average number of years to promotion for each faculty rank was consistently greater for women.[7] This bias is often extended to include more

FIGURE 2:
Medical School Faculty by Gender and Rank, 1981 and 1988
(Source: Association of American Medical Colleges; AMA Women in Medicine Study)

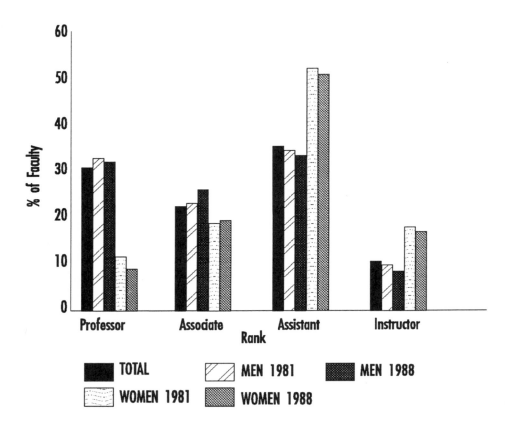

favorable review of articles published by men, more frequent approval of men's attendance at conferences, and higher ranking for men than women who present with identical qualifications.[8] This perception bias is compounded by the lack for women of palpable support systems, such as appropriate role models, mentors, schedule/tenure track flexibility, and child care.

PRACTICE CHARACTERISTICS AND ECONOMIC FACTORS

The practice characteristics of women physicians differ significantly from those of their male counterparts. In 1985, 68 percent of practicing women physicians were in the primary care field. The top five categories were internal medicine, pediatrics, general or family practice, psychiatry, and obstetrics/gynecology. In contrast, only 44 percent of male physicians practiced in these specialties.[9]

Responses to a questionnaire from 1987 medical school graduates indicate these differences are likely to persist: 68 percent of the women and 48 percent of the men planned to enter primary care fields.[10] These primary care fields tend to be those with lower prestige and lower income and those that require shorter periods of training.

Gender differences extend to the choice of practice setting. Studies from 1985 and 1986 show that 45-48 percent of women physicians choose a salaried position.[3,11] In contrast, only 23 percent of men physicians choose salaried positions, and they are often more prone to leave a salaried position after several years to go into private practice.[12] Salaried positions are beneficial because of lack of start-up costs, fixed-hour workweeks, reliable paid vacations, and lack of business concerns. The negative aspects include loss of independence and a significantly lower salary range than for self-employed physicians.

Productivity levels for women physicians are lower than for men. Data from 1983 showed that female physicians on average worked 7.9 percent fewer hours and saw 18.5 percent fewer patients than their male counterparts.[13] This trend was verified by 1988 data from the American Medical Association, which showed that women physicians work fewer hours per week than men (53.8 versus 58.7) and see fewer patients per week (109.9 vs. 122.4).[9]

Women physicians, on average, earn less from medical practice than male physicians. In 1988, the average net income for a male physician was $151,000, while that for a female was $94,900.[9]

When average incomes for men and women are compared over all levels of experience, statistically significant differences can be found. Female physicians' income increases from 57.2 percent to 82 percent of male physicians' income as years of experience increase. However, reviewing figure 3, page 22, indicates that the relative percentage gains shown by women physicians are actually the result of decreased income earned by male physicians rather than an increase in female physician income.

Lower salaries earned by women physicians apply across all specialty boundaries, as shown in figure 4, page 23.

Because women physicians work fewer hours and see fewer patients than male physicians, it could be surmised that the decreased income for women physicians is directly related to a lower productivity. However, as figure 5, page 24, clearly shows, women physicians' average net income per hour is only 75 percent of that of men physicians. When broken down by specialty (family practice, medical specialties, surgical specialties, etc.), women earn 19-30 percent less per hour than men, even in the lower paying primary care fields.

FIGURE 3:

Average Unadjusted Net Income, by Sex and Experience, 1987

(Source, AMA Center for Health Policy Research, SMS 1988 Core Survey)

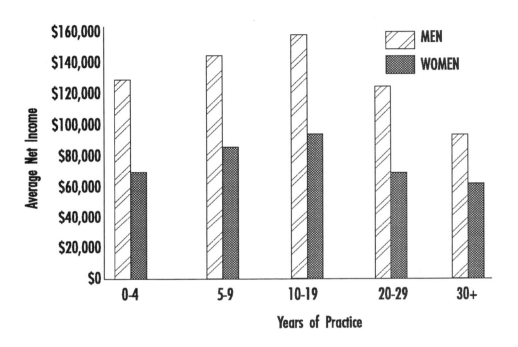

Because women physicians, as a group, are younger than their male colleagues, one might expect them to earn less. Indeed, studies from 1982 indicated that, among physicians over the age of 55, female physicians earned more than male. However, female physicians 40 or younger earned 14 percent less, and those in the 41-55 age group earned 28 percent less than their male counterparts.[13]

Because self-employed physicians earn more than salaried physicians, the earnings differential could be explained by the larger number of women who assume salaried positions as compared to men. However, in 1982, self-employed female physicians earned 18 percent less per hour than their male counter-parts, while female employee physicians earned 21 percent less per hour than males.[13]

Discrepancies in income are only partially explained by lower productivity, practice setting, and specialty choice. After correcting for these and other variables among male and female physicians, Ohsfeldt's study[14] pointed to a real income differential of 12-13 percent. In effect, this percentage acts as "an upper-bound estimate of the impact of market discrimination on the earnings of female

FIGURE 4:

Women Physicians' Average Net Annual Income as a Percentage of Male Physicians' Income, 1972 and 1982   *(Source: AMA 1983 SMS Core Survey)*

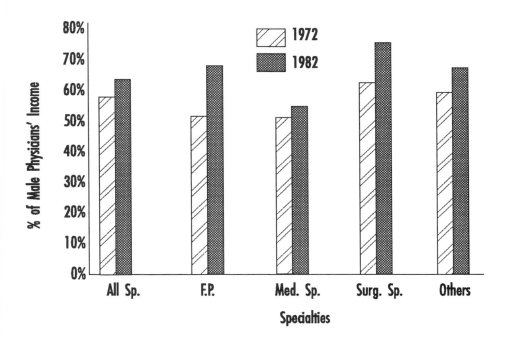

physicians."[14] In other words, for at least the past 15 years, women physicians have not been receiving equal pay for equal work.

FUTURE PROJECTIONS

The Graduate Medical Education National Advisory Committee (GMENAC) report of 1980 took a specialty-specific approach to the assessment of physician supply and demand. The report projected a surplus of 70,000 physicians in 1990 and 145,000 by the year 2000. Although the numbers were revised downward in 1983, the overall pattern of projected surpluses in most specialties did not change. Despite criticisms that have been leveled at its estimates, it has remained a standard work on which policymakers rely when they are searching for data on future medical personnel needs.

One of the many GMENAC assumptions was that the proportion of women physicians would remain constant. However, the recent increase in women entering medical schools leads to a projected proportion of women physicians of

FIGURE 5:
Women Physicians' Hourly Income as a Percentage of Male Physicians' Hourly Income, 1972 and 1982 *(Source: AMA 1983 SMS Core Survey)*

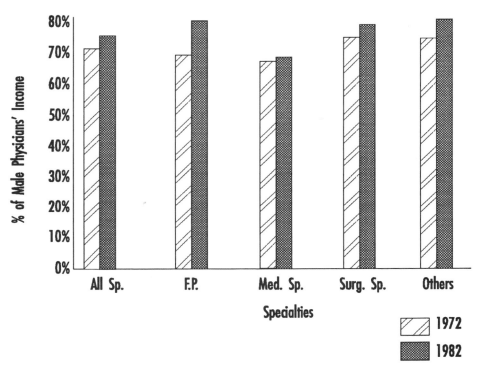

26-30 percent by the year 2000. Because of the lower number of hours worked per week by women physicians, Lanska et al.[15] concluded that the estimated physician surplus in the year 2000 (145,000 physicians) should be decreased by 28 percent (41,000 physicians).

Jacobsen and Rimm[16] adjusted the GMENAC figures even more severely to account for the increased number of women physicians, the declining enrollment in medical schools, and the decreasing productivity of physicians. They projected a surplus of only 6,000 physicians in the year 2000, with a deficit situation developing shortly after the turn of the century because of an aging population with increasing medical care demands.

In addition to changes in the total projected numbers, changes across specialty lines must also be taken into account. Women physicians tend to choose primary care specialties, as well as preventive medicine and physical/rehabilitative medicine. These specialties were initially projected by GMENAC to be in short supply or near balance. In contrast, men physicians tend to choose specialties projected to be in surplus by 1990—surgery and internal medicine subspecialties.

Thus, growing numbers of women physicians may help to alleviate potential mismatches in the nation's supply of and requirement for physicians, if current specialty choice and practice characteristics continue. However, the preference of women for urban practice locations because of spousal employment needs could exacerbate geographic maldistribution.

IMPACT FOR MANAGERS

The increasing number and percentage of women physicians will change the face of American medicine. Tending to primary care specialties that focus on the care of women and children, more willing to accept salaried positions, producing and earning less over the course of their careers—all of these factors will mitigate the high-tech, low-touch aspects of medicine and may help to curb costs.

We may see the emergence of a system similar to the Soviet model, where the vast majority of primary care physicians are women and the pay and prestige of the profession are much lower than in the United States.

Richard Restak, MD, a Washington neurologist, is particularly cynical in regards to this possibility. He feels the emphasis is on "molding physicians who are flexible, cooperative, capable of understanding group process and labor-management arbitration." These appear to be traits that would be beneficial to any manager, office-based or hospital-based, but Restak interprets them as a "lessening of power and authority" that women will tolerate much better than men. He continues, "Traditionally, women within the health professions (primarily nurses) were trained for docility and the taking of orders from superiors....These female health care workers didn't expect to make a great deal of money...nor garner much in the way of prestige....A similar situation is now developing for women doctors....Thus the quality of medical care could go down. Women will help this process. They tolerate lower income better than men. Most are in two-income families."[17]

Restak's reasoning that lower wages will result in a decrease in the quality of medical care is tenuous at best. Although he envisions the destruction of the medical profession by the influx of docile and cheap women physicians, turning medicine into a "pink ghetto" profession, others see less drastic potential. Carol Williams, MD, first woman president of the St. Louis Metropolitan Medical Society, believes that women physicians will "help physicians rediscover the relational aspects of their profession. Our pursuit of technology has been accomplished at the tremendous cost of our relationships with patients—and with each other."[18]

For managers, the increasing incidence of women physicians will mean more primary care providers who are willing to accept salaried positions. The end result will be an increase in the humanizing factors of medicine and a potential decrease in professional prestige and personal economic returns. The impact of these changes will not be fully realized for 20-30 years. Only then will we realize the full effect of the feminization of the American medical profession.

Randy S. Ellis, MD, FACEP, is Medical Director, Emergency Department, Washington County Hospital, Smithsburg, Maryland.

References

1. Friedman, E. "Women and Medicine: From Tension to Truce." *Western Journal of Medicine* 149(12):681-2, Dec. 1988.

2. Bowman, M., and Gross, M. "Overview of Research on Women in Medicine—Issues for Public Policy Makers." *Public Health Report* 101(5):513-21, Sept.-Oct. 1986.

3. Martin, S., and others. "Careers of Women Physicians: Choices and Constraints." *Western Journal of Medicine* 149(12):758-60, Dec. 1988.

4. Heins, M. "Update: Women in Medicine." *Journal of the American Medical Women's Association* 40(2):43-50, March-April 1985.

5. Gray, C. "How Will the New Wave of Women Graduates Change the Medical Profession?" *Canadian Medical Journal* 123(8):798-800,804, Oct. 18, 1980.

6. Wilson, M. "Making a Difference—Women, Medicine, and the Twenty-first Century." *Yale Journal of Biology and Medicine* 60(3):272-88, May-June 1987.

7. Wallis, L., and others. "Advancement of Men and Women in Medical Academia—A Pilot Study." *JAMA* 246(20):2350-3, Nov. 20, 1981.

8. Waxman, M. "Women in Medicine and the Medical Sciences: Problems, Progress, and Prospects." *Connecticut Medicine* 52(12):717-20, Dec. 1988.

9. *AMA Women in Medicine Project, Data Source.* Chicago, Ill.: American Medical Association, 1990.

10. *Selected Data from AAMC Medical Student Graduation Questionnaire Presented by Gender* (1987 and 1986). Washington, D.C.: Association of American Medical Colleges, 1988.

11. Zoler, M. "Salaried Physicians: Decent Money, Great Call Schedule, But..." *Medical World News* 29(2):30-2,34-6,39, Jan 25, 1988.

12. Silberger, A., and others. "Practice Characteristics of Male and Female Physicians." *Health Affairs* 6(4):104-9, Winter 1987.

13. "Differences in Practice Characteristics Between Female and Male Physicians; AMA Center for Health Policy Research." *Connecticut Medicine* 48(5):329-31, May 1984.

14. Ohsfeldt, R., and Culler, S. "Differences in Income between Male and Female Physicians." *Journal of Health Economics* 5(4):335-46, Dec. 1986.

15. Lanska, M., and others. "Effect of Rising Percentage of Female Physicians on Projections of Physicians Supply." *Journal of Medical Education* 59(11, Part 1):849-55, Nov. 1984.

16. Jacobsen, S., and Rimm, A. "The Projected Physicians Surplus Re-evaluated." *Health Affairs* 6(2):48-56, Summer 1987.

17. Restak, R. "We Need More Cheap, Docile Women Doctors." *Washington Post*, April 27, 1987.

18. Friedman, E. "Changing the Ranks of Medicine: Women MDs." *Medical World News* 29(8):57-68, April 25, 1988.

CHAPTER   3

GENDER DIFFERENCES IN
MEDICAL PRACTICE

by Linda Jean Lemay, MD

With women constituting an ever-growing percentage of physicians in the United States and Canada, more and more studies are being done to see what similarities and differences exist between male and female medical practices.

Much of the information on gender differences in medical practice comes from surveys of our Canadian colleagues. The January 1990 issue of *Medical Care* presented data collected by the University of Montreal's Department of Social and Preventive Medicine.[1] The authors note that in Canada women now make up 44 percent of medical school enrollees, only a slightly higher percentage than the U.S. figure of 37 percent. In French-Canadian medical schools, the percentage of female students is even higher—57.7 percent in 1987! Like most studies of this nature, data were collected in the form of mailed surveys, in this case to a sample of 900 general practitioners in Quebec. Of the 720 who responded, 373 were women and 347 were men.

One immediate difference noted was that the females were younger than the males, with an average age of 31.6 years compared to 38.8 years, respectively. Women were almost three times more likely men to work as salaried general practitioners in public community health centers (34.4 percent vs. 12.1 percent).

The focus of the authors here[1] was on differences in types of practices, which were consistent among males and females in both salaried and fee-for-service settings. The female practitioners were significantly less involved in emergency care, home care, and administrative work than were their male counterparts. The authors speculate that the tendency of women to limit their practices to office-based settings is due to their larger share of home and child-rearing responsibilities. Unfortunately, the survey did not specifically inquire into the amount of time spent on family duties.

No significant gender differences were observed by the authors in location of practice, mode of practice, or involvement in community health. As far as health counseling and patient education are concerned, women in private practice scored higher in these areas for both attitude and clinical practice. In the salaried group, however, no such gender differences appeared. Presumably, this was because those physicians working in public health clinics were more focused on preventive health and chose that type of practice on the basis of this interest.

Despite the gender differences found in the study, the authors note that male and female physicians may be growing less dissimilar over time. The evidence for this is in comparative data collected two years previously,[2] which showed even greater disparities than the present study in the areas of type of practice and involvement in home care. It will be interesting to see if future studies continue to reveal a narrowing gender gap in the practices of these general practitioners.

Another Canadian study of women in medicine was published in the *Journal of the Canadian Medical Association* in 1990 by the University of Toronto.[3] In this case, data from a recent national survey of 2,398 Canadian physicians (297 female and 2,101 male) were used to examine gender differences in medical practices and attitudes. It was found that women prefer group over solo practices and were overrepresented in community health centers. In contrast to the Quebec study, the women and men in this survey relied equally upon a fee-for-service structure, with about 80 percent deriving more than two-thirds of their income in this way.

Consistent with earlier research, this survey affirmed that female physicians are significantly more likely than males to enter general practice. Only one-third of the women, compared to one-half of the men surveyed, were in specialties. The most popular female specialties were psychiatry, anesthesia, internal medicine, and pediatrics. There was also a small but significant female preference for urban rather than rural practice settings.

The female physicians in this study reported working fewer hours, on average, than did their male colleagues: 38 versus 45 hours per week. (Both work significantly fewer hours than their American counterparts, however.) The Canadian women's shorter workweek seems to be due primarily to fewer hours spent in hospitals. Although the women physicians spent proportionately more time in their offices and had equivalent patient loads, they saw fewer patients per week than did the men. This may explain the significant differences in mean annual income, which was $103,100 for the men and $77,000 for the women (after expenses but before taxes).

The authors performed multiple regression analysis to determine if the differences identified in workweek and income were due to variables such as the lower average age of the female physicians, the higher numbers of male specialists, or differences in practice settings. They found that even controlling for age and specialty, males worked 7 more hours per week, on average, than did females. Of greater concern, however, is their finding that, even after adjusting for number of hours worked and for patient visits, age, and specialty, the income differences persisted! In other words, the lower income received by Canadian female physicians is not a result of their being general practitioners seeing fewer patients and working shorter hours.

No alternative explanation is offered to account for this significant income discrepancy, which has been confirmed by studies in the United States. In 1982, an AMA survey showed that, even when male and female physicians worked the same number of hours in practice, the women in private practice made 18 percent less than the men, while women in salaried positions earned 21 percent less.[4]

To compound this inequity of remuneration, women have another handicap. They continue to take on primary responsibility for home and child care even when working full time in demanding careers. A 1980 survey by the American Academy of Family Physicians of over 3,000 members showed that male physicians were six times as likely as females to have spouses who were homemakers, even when there were no children in the home.[5] With children, this difference rose to twelve-fold. This same survey confirmed the male/female income discrepancy. Even when income was examined by practice arrangement, women dominated the lower income bracket in every category examined.

The authors speculate that female physicians may spend more time per patient, and this does appear to be generally true. Langwell reports 1978 AMA data that show that, in all specialties, female physicians spend more time per patient than males.[6] The greatest differential occurred in obstetrics-gynecology. Males in this specialty saw an average of 3 patients per hour, compared to 1.73 for females. Data from the 1981 National Ambulatory Care Survey in the United States confirm that female obstetrician-gynecologists spend more time per patient than do males, averaging 17.1 versus 13.8 minutes per visit.[7] No one to date has proven that more time spent in patient interaction translates into higher quality care. However, one could hypothesize that more time spent with patients does improve patient satisfaction.

What are patient preferences for physician gender? A few studies have attempted to answer this question. A review of the literature by Weisman and Teitelbaum of John Hopkins University published in 1985[8] concluded that same-sex physician-patient interactions may be characterized by better communication and stronger rapport than dyads of opposite sexes. One author quoted in this literature survey found that female physicians tended to be more empathetic than males in dealing with conditions that are uniquely female.[9] Another study mentioned here noted that male physicians may discourage information exchange with female patients.[10] Further, the researchers found that, whereas women asked more questions than men, male physicians tended to give shorter, less technical answers to the women and attribute more psychological basis to their complaints than to men's.

A 1986 University of California study of 28 family practice residents[11] found that enhanced physician sensitivity (both self-reported and objectively observed) improved patient compliance, as measured by fewer no-show appointments. Physicians' nonverbal communication skills were also shown to be significantly related to patient satisfaction. Perhaps because only four of the residents in the study were female, the author did not attempt to draw any conclusions about the impact of physician gender on sensitivity or communication skills.

The University of Melbourne Department of Community Medicine in 1987 conducted a telephone survey of 250 women, selected at random from the telephone directory, in order to ascertain perceptions about female general practitioners.[12] The authors note that "the results indicate a much more favorable disposition by female patients towards female GPs than has been earlier reported." The majority of the respondents perceived no difference in a number of professional attributes of female and male physicians. Preference seemed to be most strongly correlated to the gender of patients' current physicians. The preference for a female physician was stronger if a gynecological examination or discussion of emotional/personal problems was involved. The authors concluded that the increasing numbers of female general practitioners were "unlikely to experience any obstacle to their full participation arising from the perceptions of their female patient" (what a relief!). Other studies have confirmed that female patients tend to prefer female physicians for pelvic examinations and intimate consultations.

So, we have evidence that female physicians are more empathetic, establish better rapport, and spend more time with patients—especially when the patients are female—and that these qualities tend to improve patient satisfaction and compliance. What, then, can be said about physician gender and its effect on the actual practice of medicine, especially as it relates to quality of care? Unfortunately, there is little information yet on this subject.

Statistics on differences in practice patterns of male and female physicians were reported in the December 1990 issue of *Academic Medicine*. In a survey of 450 physicians (364 men and 86 women) who graduated from Jefferson Medical College between 1977 and 1981, similar differences are seen in hours worked and income. Ninety-seven percent of the men were employed full time, compared to 83 percent of the women. Of the full-time practitioners, females worked a mean of 55 hours per week, while males averaged 60 hours. As far as number of patients seen per week was concerned, the average was 88 for the women and 94 for the men in full-time practice. Women were more likely than men to practice in urban, medically undeserved areas and to treat patients of lower socioeconomic status. (Although this survey did not include income, it can be safely assumed, given the last information, that women earned lower mean salaries than did the men.)

Similarities between male and female graduates from Jefferson Medical College were found in responses to questions of job satisfaction, scientific productivity, and perceived problems. Both sexes complained about having too little leisure time, a lack of time to keep up with medical literature, and a lack of time for family affairs. The men perceived more problems than the women as far as interacting with hospital administrators, oversupply of physicians, and medical malpractice litigation. These differences may reflect the higher percentage of men in the surgical specialties in this study.

In the June 1990 issue of *Medical Care*, a study of 426 health care practitioners in 16 Boston ambulatory care practices attempted to measure quality of medical care by the performance of specific tasks.[13] According to the authors, the only prior study to compare technical performance of male and female physicians, done in a pediatric setting, showed no significant gender differences. Panels of physicians, in the present study, approved eight specific tasks to be evaluated by project staff. The adult medicine tasks were: (1) follow-up of low hematocrit, (2) screening for cancer in women, (3) follow-up of elevated serum glucose, and (4) monitoring of patients on Digoxin. In the pediatric setting, areas agreed upon for study were: (1) follow-up of positive urine cultures, (2) well child care, (3) assessment of dehydration in gastroenteritis, and (4) follow-up of otitis media. Performance of task criteria was evaluated using medical record reviews, and given a score of 0 to 100, after mixed-model multivariant computer analysis.

The results of this very complex study were broken down not only by gender of patient and practitioner, but also by level of practitioner training, which included resident physicians, attending physicians, and nonphysicians. For our purposes, we will concentrate on the gender issues. Overall, few differences related to gender and role emerged. One significant difference did occur in the area of cancer screening in women, where female attending physicians performed better than the males. However, female residents did not show better performance than their male counterparts for this task. The authors speculate that more experienced female physicians become more sensitized to this role than do males (perhaps because their practices tend to have a higher percentage of women patients).

Another unexpected finding was the comparatively low scores of female residents treating urinary tract infections in children. It seems that much of this observed difference was due to overtreatment, i.e., treatment begun before confirmation of the diagnosis. The authors hypothesize that less experienced female physicians might sympathize with a patient experiencing a condition that they themselves may have experienced and might want to alleviate discomfort prior to obtaining a definitive diagnosis. An alternate hypothesis was that the women residents might have empathized with the parent bringing in the child, who most often was the mother. (The authors spend a lot of time hypothesizing instead of asking the practitioners themselves what they thought caused the practice differences.)

Two interesting patient gender effects were seen in the treatment of urinary tract infections and otitis media in children. The authors found that superior care was rendered to the gender having the greater predilection for the condition, i.e., girls for urinary tract infections and boys for otitis media. Thus, it seems, both male and female physicians play the odds; their level of suspicion rises according to known incidence of disease (not surprisingly).

For those curious as to the performance of physician-extenders, they did as well or better than the physicians in all areas except cancer screening in women, despite the fact that the vast majority of these professionals were women. The hypothetical explanation given for this is that nonphysicians have difficulty remembering preventive health measures during visits for another medical condition (the one-track mind theory). Clearly, more research needs to be done to conclude if there are significant gender differences in the quality of medical care delivered by practitioners, but this was certainly an ambitious start.

The paucity of research on female versus male physicians' medical care is probably a reflection of the few numbers of practicing women doctors in the past. Given the rising percentages of female medical students and residents in recent years, we will surely see more data published in the near future. It is encouraging that the studies to date have found few gender differences in quality of care. Even more positive is the increasing emphasis being placed, in medical training as well as literature, on the importance of interpersonal rapport to patient care. In this high-tech world, it is gratifying to see the apparently humanizing effect of the "feminization of medicine."

Linda Jean Lemay, MD, is Medical Director, Oneida City Hospital, Oneida, N.Y.

References

1.   Maheux, B., and others. "Female Medical Practitioners: More Preventive and Patient Oriented?" *Medical Care* 28(1):87-92, Jan. 1990.

2.   Maheux, B., and others. "Do Female General Practitioners Have a Distinctive Type of Medical Practice?" *Canadian Medical Association Journal* 139(8):737-40, Oct. 15, 1988.

3.   Williams, A., and others. "Women in Medicine: Practice Patterns and Attitudes." *Canadian Medical Association Journal* 143(3):194-201, Oct. 15, 1988.

4. Davis, K. "How Do Practice Styles of Men and Women Differ?" *The Internist* 27(3):10-2, March 1986.

5. Ogle, K., and others. "Gender Specific Differences in Family Practice Graduates." *Journal of Family Practice* 23(4):357-60, Oct. 1986.

6. Langwell, K. "Factors Affecting the Incomes of Men and Women Physicians: Further Explorations." *Journal of Human Resources* 17(2):261-75, Spring 1982.

7. Cypress, B. "Characteristics of Visits to Female and Male Physicians." *Vital and Health Statistics*: Series 13, No. 49, U.S. Department of Health and Human Services, Hyattsville, Md., 1980.

8. Weisman, C., and Teitelbaum, M. "Physician Gender and the Physician-Patient Relationship: Recent Evidence and Relevant Questions." *Social Science and Medicine* 20(11):1119-27, 1985.

9. Haar, E., and others. "Factors Related to the Preference for a Female Gynecologist." *Medical Care* 13(9):782-90, Sept. 1975.

10. Wallen, J., and others. "Physician Stereotypes about Female Health and Illness." *Women and Health* 4(2):135-46, Summer 1979.

11. Matter, M., and others. "Relationship of Physicians' Nonverbal Communication Skill to Patient Satisfaction." *Health Psychology* 5(6):581-94, 1986.

12. Schlicht, S., and Dunt, D. "Women's Perceptions of Female General Practitioners." *Community Health Studies* 11(3):176-82, 1987.

13. Hall, J., and others. "Performance Quality, Gender, and Professional Role. A Study of Physicians and Nonphysicians in 16 Ambulatory Care Practices." *Medical Care* 28(6):489-501, June 1990.

CHAPTER 4

WOMEN PHYSICIANS IN CAREER TRACKS

by Marianne D. Kanning, MD

CLINICAL/ACADEMIC TRACK

Physician's career paths demonstrate gender differences. Women tend to choose primary care fields and rarely enter surgery. They are paid less and are less likely to be self-employed, and they are underrepresented in positions of authority within medical organizations and academia.[1]

ACADEMIC TRACK

Academia provides a supportive and creative environment where ideas can be shared, research can be conducted, clinical medicine can be practiced, and the physicians of tomorrow are taught. The work is hard, the hours are long, and the administrative and committee responsibilities are demanding.[2] Women have always been involved in medical education, but over time it is becoming clear that as more women are opting for the academic route, more are being held to the lower ranks of the medical school faculty.[3]

Between 1978 and 1989, the number of women faculty members in US. medical schools increased 76 percent, while the male faculty increased 25 percent. At the same time, women full-time faculty rose from 15 to 20 percent. The greatest increase was in women MD-PhDs.[3] In 1989, the greatest increase in faculty rank was at the assistant professor level (140 percent). Forty-nine percent of the women faculty members now hold this rank. Associate professor or professor rank accommodated only 29 percent women, compared to 57 percent men. Since 1985, women associate professors have proportionately leveled, while professors have dropped one percentage point.[3] In 1987, almost 90 percent of the male medical school faculty was at the rank of assistant professor or higher, while the female faculty was less than 78 percent, with almost 50 percent at the assistant professor level.[2] In 1989, there were only three women deans of American medical schools.[4] By the age of 47, only 28 percent of the women have been granted the rank of full professor, compared to 61 percent of the males. The average number of years to promotion for each faculty rank was consistently greater for women.[5]

Why do women fail to ascend the academic ladder as quickly as men? Only 3 percent of the women as compared with 12 percent of the men had become professors after 12 years as faculty members.[8] Women tend to be less involved in research, require maternity leaves of absence, attempt to flex their schedules around their families' needs, and shy away from the time-consuming and very political administrative duties. Over 45 percent of the women in academic medicine with children had their first child after their training was completed, in the early phase of their academic careers.[6] Conflicts between family and career responsibilities continue as the mother returns to work. Breast feeding, day care, and the sick child present the greatest stressors to the academic women physician. Only a few of the women academicians are able to balance family and the stringent research and publication requirements of most medical schools. Most universities require a minimum number of publications within four to seven years after joining the faculty to obtain tenure.[6] This puts young faculty women, who work less than full time in order to balance family responsibilities, at a distinct disadvantage along the tenure track.

ADMINISTRATIVE TRACK

Women are underrepresented in positions of power. They are less likely than men to have positions of authority within professional and academic organizations.[7] Though women have a tendency not to join medical organizations, this is not the case in the academic setting. Thus, numbers alone are not the reason women are not in powerful positions.

Board certification provides another measure of status in the medical profession. Female physicians are less likely to be board certified; 57 percent of male physicians hold at least one board certification, in contrast to only 38 percent of female physicians.[1]

Becoming a leader in a male-dominated field is foreign to the female strengths, values, and goals. A prototype of male leadership constitutes aggressive, combative, competitive, and rough interpersonal interactions. The female style of leadership includes caring for and working with others; helping everyone to succeed. Occasionally, a female will emerge as a leader, but the female qualities of leadership emerging from a male-dominated profession seems remote. The rules for becoming a leader are male rules and not compatible with female values, communication styles, and family life. The two issues here are[8]:

- Women will not likely become leaders in medicine (the price is too high, the structure too alien).

- Those few women who do become leaders will follow the male profile.

ROLE IN ORGANIZATIONS

Friedman feels that organized medicine is wanting and seeking women physicians representatives in organized medicine. In 1988, women represented only 10.5 percent of all AMA members. Only 50.3 percent of women medical students, 32.1 percent of women residents, and 29.7 percent of young women physicians belong to this organization. Four percent of the AMA delegates in 1983 and only 9 percent in 1987 were women. Two women held state or national AMA offices in 1977, and only six held such offices in 1987. No women currently serve on the AMA Board of Trustees.[5]

Reasons for not participating in organized medicine are several:

Dual Roles. Family responsibilities make it difficult to attend the many after-hours meetings required to participate. It takes an average of a decade or two to emerge as a leader. Few women physicians have been active long enough, since many put off participation until their children are grown.[9] Because of this hiatus, women have not had the opportunity to build the power base that is essential to success.[10]

Lack of Role Models. There are few women physicians in the ranks of organized medicine to provide strong role models.[11] Lacking role models, women may fail to recognize the importance of becoming involved.[10] With the growing numbers of women in medicine comes influence and the ability to define and affect the issues in organized medicine. Women must no longer be so conscious of their position as a minority in medicine.[12] Mentor programs with medical students help advise the students as to the structure and need for participating in organized medicine.[13]

Lack of Leadership Skills Development. Without mentors, women find it difficult to learn to play the game of politics. With guidance, women physicians can build their confidence in their leadership abilities and become more effective leaders.[10]

Competition in Medical Practice. Competition in the work force finds more physicians competing for fewer positions. Women may find that they are not aggressive enough to compete successfully. Women may find it difficult to compete in organized medicine as well as clinical medicine.[10]

To be heard in organized medicine, we must first encourage all female physicians to belong at all levels. We are only as strong as our numbers represent. We must encourage our peers to accept leadership roles and then support them into elected office. Only with female involvement can organized medicine promote and protect the interests of all physicians.[11]

Marianne D. Kanning, MD, is Medical Director, St. Francis Regional Medical Center, Shakopee, Minnesota.

References

1. Martin, S., and others. "Gender and Medical Socialization." *Journal of Health and Social Behavior* 29(4):333-43, Dec. 1988.

2. Jones, E. "Moving into the Medical Organization Hierarchy." *Internist* 27(3):21-2, March 1986.

3. Whiting, B., and Bickel, J. "Women on Faculties of U.S. Medical Schools, 1978-1989." *AAMC Data Report* 65(4):277-8, April 1990.

4. Gross, L. "An Interview with Nancy E. Gary, MD, a Medical School Dean." *New York State Journal of Medicine* 90(6):321-2, June 1990.

5. Friedman, E. "Changing the Ranks of Medicine—Women MDs." *Medical World News* 29(8):57-68, April 25, 1988.

6. Levinson, W., and others. "Women in Academic Medicine—Combining Career and Family." *New England Journal of Medicine* 321(22):1511-7, Nov. 30., 1988.

7. Callan, C. "Women and Organized Medicine." *Internist* 27(3):19-22, March 1986.

8. McDonald, L. "Women Physicians and Organized Medicine." *Western Journal of Medicine* 149(6):777-8, Dec. 1988.

9. Martin, S., and others. "Careers of Women Physician—Choices and Constraints." *Western Journal of Medicine* 149(6):758-60, Dec. 1988.

10. "Women in Organized Medicine: A Call for Action." *Maryland Medical Journal* 38(9):720-1, Sept. 1989.

11. Bartuska, D. "Women in Academic Medicine—Equalizing the Opportunities." *Western Journal of Medicine* 149(6):779-80, Dec. 1988.

12. Ellis, R. "The Feminization of the American Medical Profession: Changes in the Factors of Production for the American Health Care Industry." Unpublished paper, 1989.

13. Poole, L. "The Struggle for Balance." *California Physician* 7(11):36-41, Nov. 1990.

14. Costanza, M. "Women in Medical Leadership." *Journal of the American Women's Medical Association* 44(6):185-6, Nov.-Dec. 1989.

CHAPTER 5

WHY DO WOMEN CHOOSE THE CAREERS THEY CHOOSE

by Barbara LeTourneau, MD, MBA

Women physicians tend to choose careers in clinical medicine and within clinical medicine to choose primary care as their specialty. Women are less likely to choose academic or administrative careers and advance more slowly in these areas when they are selected. It's very likely that the choice of careers has two main factors: motivators and acceptance within the career choice.

Althoughs, there is no generalization that applies to all men or all women when speaking about motivators, there are some cultural and social differences between men and women. It is very common for women to find satisfaction in their lives through social relationships. They look at their connections with others as a way to define themselves and to define the meaning in their lives. This is especially true regarding family. Mothering children is an extremely significant motivator.

Men, on the other hand, have a tendency to define themselves in terms of their relationship to society. This could be in their achievements, social status, income, goals, or job position. This is not to say that income and goals are not important to women and that social relationships are not important to men, but it has been shown many times that, even as children, women tend to be more social and collaborative and men tend to be more individual and aggressive.

The second factor is acceptance. As physicians, women are very well accepted by patients. This would lead women physicians to choose primary care or other specialties where they have a great deal of contact with patients and develop longer, more lasting relationships. Also, women are well accepted as peers in clinical settings. Women physicians tend to be seen by other physicians as competent. This was not always true, but there is little question, currently, about the clinical competence of women as physicians. However, academic and administrative medicine are different from clinical medicine. Research done by women tends to be published less often and to be taken less seriously by male colleagues. Women tend to take longer to reach professorships, and fewer women reach the higher levels of academic and administrative positions. They are given assignments of lower prestige and fewer of their own preferred projects. The usual explanation for these differences is the intensive time demands in administrative and academic medicine and their interference with the still predominantly female role in child care.

GENDER ISSUES IN JOB CHOICES

One must always keep in mind that gender issues are generalizations and that many of the issues that are attributed to one gender certainly can be issues to members of the other gender as well. Also, it should be noted that issues will be different for women who are married, women who have children, and women who are single. We've already referred to motivators and acceptance within the career field. There are numerous other issues, however, that need to be considered when one looks at the careers of women physicians.

An issue common to both men and women is hours worked. This means not only the number of hours but also the type of hours (i.e., evening hours, night hours, weekend hours, and call hours). Traditionally, child care and responsibility for managing the family and the home in our society have fallen on women. For this reason, women tend to work fewer hours.

A related issue is control over scheduling. Men, of course, also want to be available for their families, but women have more social motivation to "be there" for their children and to be able to perform the duties of mother. The need is to be available for their families not only for emergencies, but also for routinely scheduled events. This requires women to be able to plan their schedules and control them more tightly than men. Many studies have demonstrated that male physicians are more likely to have spouses who stay home on a full-time or part-time basis to perform homemaker and child care duties. This frees men to devote more time and energy to their careers.

A third issue is income. Income of women of the same age and specialty when compared to men tends to be lower even when adjusted for hours worked and patients seen. Although the reasons for the income differences are not clear, they are a factor in the choice of careers. For women who are married to spouses who also work, a lower income might be an acceptable trade-off for more control over schedule or hours to support a more flexible life-style. For women who are single parents or have no spouses or children, a need for higher income might be accompanied by a willingness and ability to give up some control over the schedule. This issue tends to be more variable for women and more negotiable than it is for men.

A final factor, unrelated to hours, scheduling, and income, is personal satisfaction with career. We believe that women will select and stay in a job in which they feel that their personal needs are important in the workplace. Their personal needs will relate not only to their schedules and income, but also to their individual acceptance and support. This could also include their growth as persons but it involves more with whom they work and the culture of the workplace. This will include a collegial atmosphere with other physicians, a collaborative relationship with other clinic or ancillary personnel, and a culture of supportiveness in the workplace. This type of an atmosphere, which fosters growth as a person and in a career, is extremely important to women.

Finally, a significant gender issue is the ability of a woman to rise in an organization if she so desires. Many women are content with a clinical practice or an academic or administrative practice that would stay the same for a very long time. However, among those women who would like to take on more responsibility, it is very important that the management of the organization give clear indications that women are allowed to move up. In taking a job in an organization, whether it is clinical, academic, or administrative, men presume that, if they demonstrate merit and interest, they will rise to the top. Women, however, realize that demonstrating merit is not enough, that unless an atmosphere exists within the organization to foster the growth of women, they have no career ladder. Most often this will relate to altering career paths to meet the needs of those individuals who are involved in child-rearing for a number of years. It also will involve being alert to expressions of interest by women to be involved in the organization and fostering that interest, even if the time commitment is small at first. Finally, it involves taking the time and interest to teach women "the ropes" regarding how things get done in the organization.

ISSUES OF TURNOVER

As increasing numbers of women become physicians, it will be important to be able to attract women into the organization or risk having a smaller pool of physicians from which to choose. Once these physicians are hired into the organization, it's imperative to try to avoid turnover. Turnover is a very costly fact of life in many organizations. Even if turnover is not related to firing or layoffs, it creates a feeling of unrest and instability within the organization. When physicians leave clinics or businesses, they often leave to go to a different clinic in a similar area. The previous employer will lose patients who choose to follow their physician rather than stay at the clinic and get new physicians. Women physicians have a tendency to form stronger relationships with their patients, and this may cause more patients to leave and follow a woman physician into a new practice than would follow a man.

People leave clinics for a variety of reasons. Some gender issues in turnover cannot be avoided. For example, a woman may quit her job to follow a spouse who has been transferred out of town. This tends to occur more with female physicians and is probably unavoidable. Women sometimes convert to part-time practice after they have children or quit clinical practice altogether when their children are young. It is debatable whether this type of turnover can be avoided, although it may be possible to retain these physicians as part-time employees if their child care needs can be met.

An important way to prevent turnover is to meet the family needs of physicians, both men and women. As mentioned earlier, because of the cultural and social roles of women in our society, women tend to be the nurturers and the primary care givers within their families. This is especially true of single parents. Because of the cultural training of women to be mothers and nurturers, even career-oriented women will have strong needs to nurture their families. Although more and more men are also becoming extremely involved with their families, it is uncommon for men to feel that they are the primary nurturers and it is less common for men to feel the extreme guilt that women feel when they are not able to provide for their families' emotional needs. Some recent innovations to meet family needs are on-site child care, flexible hours, and flexibility in tenure and administrative tracks. More and more companies are either providing child care on the work site or developing agreements with child care corporations to provide child care for employees. This could include financial subsidies for child care, but, for most physicians, the financial cost is not the major issue. The major issue is finding competent child care. Assisting with child care could even include a recruiting program for in-home child care or a string of in-home nannies that is retained by the organization for hiring by employees. Many clinics and hospitals are also beginning to provide subsidized sick child care to reduce absenteeism for parents caring for ill children.

In preventing turnover, one must also look at the career goals of the individual physician. If a physician is interested in taking on administrative responsibilities or doing certain types of clinical research, it is in the interest of the organization to actively give responsibility to these people if they are qualified. If people are not yet qualified to move up or take on new responsibilities, the organization should offer them training or guide them to decisions regarding how they can become better qualified. This need not necessarily mean financial support while they get training, but if there are certain goals specific to the individual, they should be encouraged to undergo the training etc.

Often, especially in administrative medicine and academic medicine, the "good ol' boy club" operates. Men, as the top managers, unwittingly give assignments and responsibility to other men whom they know are competent or have an interest. This might even include such simple or powerful things as committee assignments. Women may be less verbal about these types of interests, but this type of goal should be sought out by managers, perhaps in a performance evaluation. Women thus identified can be kept in mind and actively solicited for responsibilities matching their interests. Because most managers are male, the tendency to be connected to other men at the workplace must be thoughtfully offset by active monitoring and involvement to seek out the interests of women physicians. Women who feel that their needs and their personal motivators are being considered are much more likely to stay with the organization even if they are somewhat unsatisfied. This is partly because of relationships that women will have developed within the organization.

Flexible hours also are important in meeting the family needs of physicians. Women who are able to adjust their hours based on the hours of their spouses and children are much more likely to stay, even if their careers are put on hold. Women will make this sacrifice because being able to meet the needs of their families at certain stages in the child-rearing process is an important gender issue. Flexible hours will also include control over the schedule and quick availability in family emergencies. Women, more than men, want to be available for family emergencies. If there are office contingencies for rescheduling patients and changing schedules because of short-term needs for child care, this will provide better job satisfaction for women.

A final gender issue in preventing turnover is sensitivity to the different styles of women. Women in general tend to be more people-oriented and more sensitive to the needs of the people around them. They will develop relationships in the workplace based on personal friendships and will tend to have a support system within the workplace. In order to retain women physicians, especially in academic and administrative settings, the organizational culture must be made friendlier to that style. This is especially crucial in these two settings, because they still tend to be male dominated, with a very strong work ethic and less of a family ethic. This demands grueling schedules and leaves less time for the interpersonal style of managing, which is characteristic of women. When organizational cultures can be made friendly to that style, women will achieve greater success as administrators and as academics and resignations will decrease. This will most likely involve altering the tenure track and management advancement so that moving more slowly during the child care years is acceptable for both men and women.

Along the same lines, women get a great deal of support from other women and tend to develop support systems in the workplace. Most women also have support systems outside of the workplace. Where there are other women who seem willing, women will tend to share their personal feelings and their goals and relationships. In order to retain women physicians, organizations should encourage the development of this type of support system. Women can be placed together on important committees so that they have a chance to work together and don't feel isolated from each other. Committees and groups can be formed to address women's problems. For example, call-sharing groups could be developed and actively promoted, as well as babysitting co-ops, patient liaison committees, and other such activities that support the needs and interests of women. This does not mean that men should be excluded from these activities, but many men will have fewer needs in these areas. When men show the interest and need for these groups and committees, they should also be encouraged to participate.

CONCLUSION

Much has been made of the "glass ceiling" in organizations. This is more prevalent in academic and administrative careers than in clinical careers. However, in certain types of clinical careers, such as orthopedic surgery and general thoracic surgery, there are few women, and these are among the highest paid and most prestigious specialties. One could say that a glass ceiling exists there too. Many statistics indicate that few women advance to the top in academic, administrative, or clinical medicine. In the American College of Physician Executives, an organization extremely sensitive to women's issues, only about 5 percent of the members are women, and only one woman physician executive, the editor of this monograph, is currently in a position of power within the organization. I think as managers we need to look at why this is true.

Certainly, many women limit their careers to easily scheduled hours that leave them adequate time to nurture their children and their spouses. This gives them control over their schedules, and they are willing to take a trade off in income. It also leaves little time for committee and organized medicine. This is an important factor in the absence of women in positions of responsibility and power. However, it is also plain that women who have willingly chosen careers without flexible hours, with very undesirable hours, or with little control over scheduling have difficulty moving up. It is doubtful that they are less competent than their male counterparts or do not desire these jobs or assignments. It is more likely that this is due to differences in management style, lack of mentors, and the natural inclination of men to go to friends and colleagues whom they know well (i.e., other men) when there are key jobs or assignments to be filled.

The best way to correct these inequities is for leaders to actively solicit participation from their female employees and actively mentor women. We must ask ourselves when there are assignments to committees, promotions to be made, or projects to be done, who would be good at this and whose goals will it meet—male and female. If women are not specifically included and sought out, they will continue to be excluded. In addition, traditional career paths, such as tenure tracks, training programs, and administrative tracks, must be made more flexible to meet differing sets of needs. Once again, unless specific efforts are made to include different needs and motivators, women will continue to be excluded. As women become more and more visible above the glass ceiling, that ceiling will melt away.

Women leaders have not been sufficiently supportive of each other in the past. Some of us have been intimidated into not helping other women within the system. We walk several fine lines, balancing work and family and also the line between being seen as too oriented toward "feminine" issues or not sympathetic enough to traditional female roles or issues. We must all actively solicit women physicians at all levels of clinical, academic, and administrative practice to mentor and train. It is only through this type of active assistance and flexibility within organizations that gender issues for female physicians can begin to be addressed.

Barbara LeTourneau, MD, MBA, is Medical Director, Emergency Department, Unity Medical Center, Fridley, Minnesota.

CHAPTER 6

FEMALE PHYSICIANS AND
HUMAN RESOURCE ISSUES

by Chris B. Emmons and
Kathleen Yaremchuk, MD, MSA

INTRODUCTION

The shortage of skilled employees and the increase in the number of minorities and women entering the workforce anticipated by the year 2000 may already have arrived. A survey of human resource professionals with 645 companies conducted by the Hudson Institute and Towers and Perrin revealed that, at 66 percent of the firms surveyed, approximately 15 percent of employees are members of minority groups; at 75 percent of the companies, at least 33 percent of the employees are women; and 12 percent of the employers had more than 50 percent of their employees aged 40 years or older. The early development of these trends has many human resource professionals expressing concern with hiring and managing diverse groups, taking care of the special needs of women, and dealing with employee shortages.[1]

The impact of these issues can be illustrated by the expanding role of women in medicine. In 1989, female physicians constituted almost 17 percent of the total physician population. This is a fourfold increase from the 1970s. Currently, 40 percent of medical students are women, with projections for this percentage to increase.

The growth of women in the medical profession is concentrated in the younger age groups, which are more likely to be involved with issues related to child bearing and child care. Maternity leave during medical school, residency, or the early years of practice is an important concern. The needs of these physicians must be met before they can participate fully in the medical profession.

This chapter discusses the issues affecting women employed in health care facilities from the initial interview to workplace environmental issues (such as sexual harassment, maternity leave, child care, and alternative work schedules) to the ability to obtain promotions.

EMPLOYMENT PRACTICES AND EQUAL EMPLOYMENT OPPORTUNITY

Title VII of the federal Civil Rights Act of 1964 prohibits discrimination in employment on the basis of race, color, religion, sex, or national origin. This is the broadest of the equal employment opportunity laws and covers recruitment, hiring, compensation, conditions of employment, discharges, job assignments, training programs, and promotions. This law applies whenever a woman is interviewed for employment, promotion, reassignment, or termination. Improper interview techniques or practices can trigger discrimination charges, and the penalties for violation of the law can be severe. In addition to legal fees, substantial back pay awards, wage adjustments, and other financial penalties are possible under this law.

The Equal Employment Opportunity Commission (EEOC) is the federal agency created by the Act to enforce its provisions. EEOC has the authority to conduct investigations of employers and to file lawsuits against employers.

In 1965 and 1967, President Lyndon B. Johnson issued Executive Orders 11246 and 11375. These orders describe the equal opportunity responsibilities of companies that bid on or hold contracts from the U.S. government. The Department of Labor was given the major administrative responsibility for these Executive Orders and established the Office of Federal Contract Compliance Programs (OFCCP) to enforce the regulations.[2]

The largest single payer of hospital expenses is the U.S. Government, through Medicare reimbursement and educational subsidies. For this reason, hospitals are subject to audit by the OFCCP regarding employment practices for professional and support staff. Hiring and promotional statistics are frequently analyzed by the OFCCP for evidence of discrimination. Interviewer's notes on employment decisions can be reviewed. If the OFCCP concludes that women have been denied employment or promotional opportunities based on improper interviewing practices, it can initiate enforcement proceedings against the employer. When recruiting, mangers and administrators should be aware of possible female underutilization in their organization's work force and the specific new hire, transfer, or promotional commitments the organization might have made to the government.

The penalties for violating these Executive Orders include cancellation, termination, or suspension in whole or in part of the contract. In addition, the Secretary of Labor or the contracting agency can recommend to the EEOC or the

Department of Justice that appropriate proceedings be instituted under Title VII of the Civil Rights Act of 1964. Both the EEOC and the OFCCP have written guidelines on employee selection procedures that apply to both informal and structured job interviews. Of major importance is the concept that women can only be disproportionately excluded from hire, transfer, or promotion for demonstrably job-related reasons.

Equal employment opportunity begins before the interview, as it is essential that women be included in the applicant pool. Frequently, the interviewer is not the person directly responsible for the employer's recruitment program. However, the interviewer should give as much advance notice as possible to those accountable for the recruitment effort in order to allow sufficient time for the identification of qualified females.

Accurate job descriptions that specify the critical components of the position are essential from the perspective of being an effective interviewer and staying in compliance with EEO law. The possibility of overtime, irregular schedules, or other requirements of the job should be stated.

An effective interviewer always starts the interview by establishing a cordial and relaxed relationship with the applicant. Once a positive relationship is established, the interviewer should ask only job-related questions regarding previous work experience, training, level of performance, and career goals. It is illegal to ask an applicant for marital or child-bearing status. The number of children a woman has, whether or not she is a single parent, her child care arrangements, or her plans for future pregnancies cannot be asked during interviews. An applicant who is questioned in such a manner has grounds for filing a lawsuit if she fails to secure the position. The applicant may not have been the best qualified for the position, but errors committed during the interview may lead to a successful lawsuit.

The applicant can be asked questions in a manner that will answer the question of availability yet not compromise the law. For example, "Are there any personal issues that may occur that will prevent you from fulfilling the requirements of the position?" is allowable and provides all the information an employer needs to know. The applicant can then choose to accept or reject the position based on how it would suit her personal situation. The decision is removed from the employer, and the need to second-guess the support system or the motivation of the applicant is eliminated. An effective interviewer does not overlook candidates who can make a contribution to the organization because their personal characteristics might be different from those of other job holders. Questions that can and cannot be asked are listed in the figure on pages 63-66.

Closing the interview properly is extremely important. It is the interviewer's responsibility to clearly explain to the applicant the status of her application. If the interviewer has concluded that the applicant is unqualified for the job, the applicant should be told this in a manner that does not insult or provoke the rejected applicant. Such applicants should be told that, if through additional work experience or training they qualify for the job in question in the future, they should reapply and their interest would be welcomed. If what the applicant can do to secure a future opportunity is discussed, any tendency for an applicant to perceive the interview as discriminatory will be reduced. If the applicant is qualified, she should be told this, as well as be given an indication of the approximate number of additional applicants who are being considered. Such information helps structure the applicant's expectations so that a refusal to offer the opportunity will not be incorrectly perceived by the applicant as being the result of discrimination. All applicants should be thanked for showing an interest in the organization and for coming in for the interview. Those still under consideration should be told how and approximately when the company will notify them regarding a final decision.

At the conclusion of every interview, the interviewer should complete a short written summary of the applicant's qualifications for the job. Proper interviewing records documenting qualifications of each candidate in job-related terms is essential when evaluating the selection decision and in ensuring that the organization has operated within the law.[2]

PERFORMANCE APPRAISALS

Performance appraisals are an important tool in maintaining and improving productivity. If properly conducted, the appraisal can improve the existing level of performance, ensure the employee is working toward organizational goals, develop women for promotions, and provide the data needed to make and defend personnel decisions.

Personnel decisions made by managers on the basis of a performance appraisal may be overturned by the courts if the method has not been shown to be job-related or valid; if the content of the performance appraisal has not been developed from an accurate job description; if the appraiser has not been able to consistently observe the employee performing her work; if the appraisal has been based on subjective or vague factors; if racial, sexual, age, or other biases of the appraiser may have influenced the appraisal; and if appraisals disputed by the employee cannot be appealed to a higher level of management for review.

As a result, performance should be evaluated against direct measures of an employee's results, and criteria should be as objective and quantitative as possible. Therefore, the first step in the performance appraisal process is to establish the criteria against which the employee will be measured. These criteria should be developed at the beginning of the performance cycle and be based on the job description. The criteria include the performance objectives and the relevant weight or priority of each objective. The strengths and weaknesses of the employee as well as any developmental needs may be considered in developing the objectives. It is advisable to obtain the employee's input at this stage of the process in order to ensure understanding and commitment. Performance appraisals typically have objectives set in the areas of job knowledge, work quality, level of activity, organizational ability, communication skills (oral and written), relationships with customers or co-workers, and special projects.

During the review period, the supervisor should provide feedback to the employee on an informal basis to correct problems; discuss changes in priority; and to reinforce positive contributions. This coaching keeps the goals in front of the employee and minimizes surprises or conflicts during the formal performance appraisal meeting.

At the end of the review cycle, the manager evaluates all relevant materials, such as operating reports, customer or co-worker feedback, and special projects or significant accomplishments. The entire review period should be considered, and the feedback should focus on results as well as the behavior observed in obtaining those results. The completed appraisal should be in writing and be reviewed to ensure against bias. Once the document is complete and an overall rating has been determined, the appraisal is discussed with the employee. Comments from the employee should be welcomed. Improvement strategies may be suggested during this performance appraisal meeting.

After the performance appraisal is completed, the process is repeated, beginning with the first step of establishing and communicating objectives.

TERMINATIONS

More than 25,000 wrongful discharge cases are pending in state and federal courts, according to a 1989 study conducted for the Bureau of National Affairs.

Employees should not be terminated until upper management has reviewed their performance and given them a chance to tell their sides of the story. Employee performance should be documented, along with proof that employees are given a chance to improve before being fired. Defenses against dismissal actions often are hampered by inaccurate performance evaluations and documentation.

When a performance problem is identified, a suggested approach is to place the employee on a performance improvement plan that describes the performance deficiencies, the results or behavior desired by management, the action management will take to assist the employee (if any), the action the employee will take to correct the problem, and the deadline by which the problem must be solved. The deadline for a performance improvement plan is based on the employee's length of service and the severity of the performance issue. Generally, 90 days is an appropriate deadline, with appraisals being documented and discussed with the employee during two 30-day intervals.

If termination is determined to be the best approach, it is important to conduct the termination interview using language that could not be interpreted as discriminatory, while being as humane as possible. If a problem is expected, a voluntary release in exchange for extra severance pay may be appropriate. Offering outplacement assistance and other job search support may also be advisable.

SEXUAL HARASSMENT

Solicitation of a sexual relationship from an employee is a violation of Title VII of the Civil Rights Act of 1964. Solicitation can vary from "innocent" jokes and innuendos to physical attacks. In 1980, the federal government issued written guidelines dealing with sexual harassment. During the following year, 1,000 sex discrimination charges alleging sexual harassment were filed. By 1983, the number quadrupled, and currently the number is stable at around 5,000 new cases a year.[3]

In 1990, the American Medical Association adopted a policy encouraging the Accreditation Council for Graduate Medical Education (ACGME) to incorporate into the "General Requirements" of the "Essentials of Accredited Residencies in Graduate Medical Education" the requirement that all residency training institutions develop a written grievance procedure that addresses sexual harassment and exploitation between educators and medical trainees and urge all medical schools to address sexual harassment and exploitation between educators and medical trainees.[4]

Sexual harassment is an expense that industry cannot afford. It costs in terms of legal expenses and settlements. It costs when work-time is lost to gossip and when rumors envelop the workplace. (Sexual harassment is seldom kept secret.) It costs in terms of lowered productivity, absenteeism, and increased employee turnover. Under the federal law, companies are financially responsible for sexual harassment by their managers and supervisors. The company is financially responsible for hourly employees if knowledge of sexual harassment existed.

Title VII sexual harassment cases involve a financial award against the company for lost wages suffered by the claimant. It is customary for the victim to have resigned from the job as a result of harassment. The loss of wages would represent a claim for full wages from the time of termination to the date comparable employment is secured. This compensation is termed a back pay award. For example, an employee earns $25,000 a year and resigns because of sexual harassment. Assume the claimant wins the suit. If the claimant was out of work for two years, the company would be liable for $50,000 in back pay, legal interest, and attorney's fees and costs. In a case involving many witnesses, it is not unusual for these costs to range between $50,000 and $100,000.

Total Cost

Claimant back pay	$ 50,000
Claimant legal fees	50,000
Claimant legal interest (8 percent)	4,000
Defendant legal fees	50,000
	$154,000

The intangible costs previously mentioned—lowered productivity, employee morale, and employee turnover—should also be considered. While sexual harassment typically occurs with a female victim and a male harasser, changes in society have transpired and charges of sexual harassment by males are becoming apparent.

To protect an organization from these charges, policies regarding harassment should be evident and widely distributed. All employee complaints should be treated in a serious manner. Established policies should be followed. Confidentiality should be observed to prevent harm to the reputation of an innocent person.

To protect oneself from such charges, avoid being alone with such employees. Keep records of work performance and make sure company officials or legal counsel are aware of potential problems.

If you are the victim of harassment, document episodes in a written diary kept at home. Discuss the incidents with co-workers discreetly and see if there are patterns of harassment. If possible, find witnesses or others suffering from similar harassment. Keep copies of all work evaluations to document satisfactory work habits prior to harassment.

Once this has been done, complain in writing to the employer. In a large organization, the complaint may need to be sent simultaneously to the corporate and regional human resource offices. Charges of discrimination can then be filed with an attorney and/or the federal Equal Employment Opportunity Commission (EEOC).

MATERNITY LEAVE

Each year thousands of women report that they are harassed, demoted, transferred, or fired after telling their managers that they are pregnant, even though the Pregnancy Discrimination Act makes it illegal to treat women differently because of pregnancy, childbirth, or related medical conditions.

Complaints about pregnancy discrimination account for 30 percent of the calls received by the 9 to 5 Job Survival Hotline, which is run by the National Association of Working Women.

Residency is at best a period of arduous, exhausting work. While the work shifts that resident physicians could be required to perform in the past were essentially uncontrolled, recent legislative changes (as in New York) have led many areas to restrict residents' hours on duty. An article in the *New England Journal of Medicine* reports that the long hours, physically exhausting work, and high levels of stress have little effect on pregnancies of medical residents compared with a control group of wives of residents.[5,6] However, the needs of pregnant residents are evidenced by the frequent lack of maternity leave policy at training hospitals.

A 1990 survey conducted by the American Medical Association Women in Medicine Advisory Panel indicated that 75 percent of the 1,200 program directors contacted have standard policies for granting maternity leave.[7] The directors were evenly divided on whether maternity leave is granted in addition to vacation, personal, or sick leave. About half of the directors said they use a combination of one or more of four types of leave (vacation, sick, disability, and maternity) to grant leave time. Only 21 programs reported exclusive use of a maternity leave category.

Time of maternity leave varies from several weeks to, in one case, a full year. Approximately one-third of the responding programs allow between four and six weeks, 25 percent allow less than four weeks, and 40 percent allow more than 6 weeks.

In this same survey, 1,165 female physicians responded regarding maternity leave. Two-thirds said they were in private practice and the rest in graduate training. Almost 74 percent of the residents and 53 percent of the practicing physicians said the established policy at their institutions allows six weeks or less for a single leave. Half of the residents and practicing physicians who had taken maternity leave while in their current practice or training program said they returned 7 to 12 weeks after giving birth; one-third waited 4 to 6 weeks; 5.7 percent of residents and 7.2 percent of the practicing physicians took 1 to 3 weeks of maternity leave. Although the usual duration is 6 to 8 weeks, the American College of Obstetricians and Gynecologists in its 1974 statement of policy on pregnancy upholds that, as with other disabilities, duration of leave should be determined by the woman's physician based on the woman's medical condition.

The 1978 amendments to the Civil Rights Act of 1964 provides the basis for maternity leave policy. Discrimination in employment related to pregnancy is unlawful sex discrimination. Pregnancy, childbirth, or related medical conditions are to be treated the same as other disabilities, including health coverage, sick leave, or disability plans. Employers may not force women to stop working when they can continue according to their physician. Arbitrary time limits for maternity leave may not be in effect if there are none for other disability leaves.

The "General Requirements" of the ACGME Essentials of Accredited Residencies do not directly address maternity leave for residents. The ACGME is now reviewing a draft to specify that programs must provide residents with "institutional policy on leave that is in compliance with federal and state laws," and a written statement of policy concerning the effect of leaves of absence, for any reason, on satisfying the criteria for completion of a residency program.

The requirements of the medical specialty boards of the American Board of Medical Specialties influence the development and implementation of maternity leave policies in residency programs. The board policies determine amount of time allowed annually for leave to be eligible to sit for board examinations. A 1987 survey of specialty boards revealed a wide range of general leave policies, with no specific accommodations for maternity leave. Consensus between ACGME and the American Board of Medical Specialties needs to occur to facilitate maternity leave policy.

Health care institutions need to have established policies relating to:

- Maternity leave

- Birth and adoption

- Category of leave credited (sick, vacation, maternity, unpaid leave, short term disability)

- Paid or unpaid leave

- Provision for continuation of insurance benefits during leave and payment of premiums

- Accrual of sick leave and vacation time

CHILD CARE

In 1947, only 19 percent of U.S. mothers worked outside of the home; by 1987 that figure had risen to 65 percent. It is expected that the figure will continue to increase, reaching 80 percent by the year 2000. As the percentage of women with children in the labor pool grows, companies offering child care benefits will have a competitive advantage. During the 1980s, there was significant growth in employer-supported child care, but it still only involves 12 percent of the 44,000 employers with more than 100 employees.

In September 1989, the Women in Medicine Advisory Panel to the Board of Trustees of the American Medical Association initiated a survey of U.S. hospitals to determine the existence and characteristics of child care services available to resident and staff physicians, medical students, nurses, and hospital employees. Hospitals were divided into community and community teaching hospitals. Questionnaires or interviews were completed by 1,481 hospitals, yielding a response rate of 88.5 percent.[8] One hospital reported having had a program since 1942, and more than 80 percent reported programs beginning in the 1980s. Thirty-five percent of the teaching hospitals reported having child care facilities available, whereas the figure is half that for community hospitals. When asked if there were plans to develop child care programs in hospitals not currently offering services, 14 percent in both groups answered affirmatively.

Hospitals providing child care services were asked who was eligible for participation. The programs appear to be directed at nurses, nonmedical staff, and others. Residents and medical students may be least likely to participate. Issues limiting participation by physicians and medical students relate to waiting lists that were reported as existing at hospital programs, and fees that range from zero to as high as $160 per week. Limited hours are also a problem; 24 percent of community hospitals and 20 percent of teaching hospitals had child care programs that were open on Saturdays, Sundays, or holidays. Only 5 percent of community hospital programs and 3 percent of teaching hospital programs were open 24 hours.

About 85 percent of programs accept children from 6 weeks to 5 years of age. However, these programs are most likely to have waiting lists (41 to 61 percent, depending on age and community versus teaching hospital program). Before- and after-school programs for children over five are available at 53 percent of centers.

Hospitals offering such services believe child care is a helpful tool for recruiting, and the majority of hospitals believe it reduces absenteeism among employees.

St Joseph's Hospital in Marshfield, Wisconsin, is a 524-bed facility with 2,200 employees. In a town of 20,000, the hospital opened an on-site day care center in 1981. In 1990, it expanded to double its capacity to 130 children during the day and 50 in the evening and extend its hours until midnight. It accepts children up to the age of 12 and can accommodate sick children.[9] The hospital subsidizes half of the cost of placing a child in the center, and an informal sliding fee scale is used, taking into account the employee's wages and the number of children enrolled in the center.

Even with the recent size increase, the center has a waiting list of six to nine months, which limits its effectiveness as a recruiting tool. It does, however, decrease job turnover and absenteeism, results that confirm the findings of studies on employer-supported day care.[10]

An example of a firm that has addressed the need for employer-supported day care is Riverside Medical Center, Kankakee, Ill., which opened a day care center in July 1989. The medical center provides the space, utilities, maintenance, food, and equipment for the day care facility, which cares for children between the ages of six weeks and six years. Since opening the day care center, Riverside also has achieved the predicted higher employee morale, enhanced recruiting results, and lower rates of absenteeism.

Employers have become concerned with the absences created by parents staying home with sick children. In addition to creating sick child care centers and in-home services, employers are revising their sick leave policies to permit employees to stay home with sick children. A recent Conference Board survey of 521 large companies found that two-thirds of large companies offered sick leave for family members, although 59 percent of the sick leave was unpaid.

SHARED POSITIONS

Most professions recognize the need for providing part-time positions, and it is generally accepted that graduate studies can proceed at rates that vary according to the student's situation. While medical schools allow for an academic pace that is slower than the norm, residency programs are a different matter.

The hours required during residency vary from 40 to 120 hours a week. This extensive time commitment limits participation by individuals with other personal needs that need to be met. Residents with families realize that, for three to five years, 100-hour workweeks will strain marital relations and significantly limit participation in raising children. Because of these concerns, the idea of shared residency positions became popular.[11]

A shared residency position is defined as "training that is shared by two individuals and in which each individual engages in at least two-thirds but not more than three-quarters of the total training prescribed; receives for each year an amount of credit toward certification equal to the amount of training engaged in; receives at least half the salary; and receives all appropriate employee benefits." Shared schedule positions in residency programs were mandated for family practice, general pediatrics, general obstetrics and gynecology by Section 709 of the U.S. Health Profession's Educational Assistance Act of 1976. This effects all programs receiving any government funding. In 1990, 14 percent of residency programs reported part-time or shared residencies. Over half of these positions were in family practice, internal medicine, pediatrics, psychiatry, and child psychiatry.

The National Resident Matching Program (NRMP) reported that 50 programs advertised shared residencies last year. Students applying for these positions must find their own cohort and apply together. Although there are more than 50 programs with shared positions, details for each are worked out on an individual basis. Because shared residency positions are so rare, finding someone to share a position in a mutually acceptable manner is extremely difficult.

The American Medical Women's Association (AMWA) has created clearing-houses for students interested in pursuing shared residency positions. As inquiries increase, program directors will further evaluate options for reduced schedule residency programs.

Chris B. Emmons is President, Human Resource Professionals, Detroit, Michigan. Kathleen Yaremchuk, MD, MSA is Associate Medical Director for the Henry Ford Medical Group, Detroit, Michigan.

LIMITATIONS OF PREEMPLOYMENT INQUIRIES

SUBJECT AREA	LAWFUL INQUIRIES	UNLAWFUL INQUIRIES
Name	Applicant's full name.	Original name of an applicant whose name has been changed by a court order or otherwise.
	Have you ever worked for this company under a different name?	Applicant's maiden name.
	Is any additional information relative to a different name necessary to check work record? If yes, explain.	
Address or Duration of Residence	How long a resident of this state or city?	
Birthplace		Birthplace of applicant. Birthplace of applicant's parents, spouse, or other close relatives.
Age*	Are you 18 years old or older?	How old are you? What is your date of birth?

* This question may be asked only for the purpose of determining whether applicants are of legal age for employment.

Subject Area	Lawful Inquiries	Unlawful Inquiries
Religion or Creed		Inquiry into an applicant's religious denomination, religious affiliations, church, parish, pastor, or religious holidays observed. An applicant may not be told "This is a Catholic, Protestant, or Jewish organization."
Race or Color		Complexion or color of skin.
Photograph		Requirement that an applicant for employment affix a photograph to an employment application form. Request an applicant, at his or her option, to submit a photograph. Requirement for photograph after interview but before hiring.
Height		Inquiry regarding applicant's height.
Weight		Inquiry regarding applicant's weight.

Subject Area	Lawful Inquiries	Unlawful Inquiries
Marital Status		Requirement that an applicant provide information regarding marital status or children. Are you single or married? Do you have any children? Is your spouse employed? What is your spouse's name?
Sex		Mr., Miss, or Mrs. or an inquiry regarding sex. Inquiry as to the ability to reproduce or advocacy of any form of birth control.
Health	Do you have any impairments, (physical, mental, or medical) that would interfere with your ability to do the job for which you have applied? Inquiry into contagious or communicable diseases that may endanger others. If there are any positions for which you should not be considered or job duties you cannot perform because of a physical or mental handicap, please explain.	Requirement that women be given pelvic exams.

SUBJECT AREA	LAWFUL INQUIRIES	UNLAWFUL INQUIRIES
Citizenship	Are you a citizen of the United States?	Of what country are you a citizen?
	If not a citizen of the United States, does the applicant intend to become a citizen of the United States?	Whether an applicant is naturalized or a native born citizen. The date when the applicant acquired citizenship.
	If you are not a United States citizen, have you the legal right to remain permanently in the United States?	Whether applicant's parents or spouse are naturalized of the United States. The date when such parent acquired citizenship.
National Origin	Inquiry into languages applicant speaks and writes fluently.	Inquiry into applicant's lineage, ancestry, national origin, descent, parentage, or nationality.
		Nationality of applicant's parents or spouse.
		What is your mother tongue?
		Inquiry into how applicant acquired ability to read, write, or speak a foreign language.

Subject Area	Lawful Inquiries	Unlawful Inquiries
Education	Inquiry into the academic, vocational, or professional education of an applicant and public and private schools attended.	
Experience	Inquiry into work experience.	
Arrests	Have you ever been convicted of a crime? If so, when, where, and nature of offense? Are there any felony charges pending against you?	Inquiry regarding arrests.
Relatives	Names of applicant's relatives, other than a spouse, already employed by this company.	Address of any relative of applicant, other than address (within the United States) of applicant's father and mother, husband or wife, and minor dependent children.
Notice in Case of Emergency	Name and address of person to be notified in case of emergency.	Name and address of nearest relative to be notified of emergency.

SUBJECT AREA	LAWFUL INQUIRIES	UNLAWFUL INQUIRIES
Military Experience	Inquiry into an applicant's military experience in the Armed Forces of the United States or in a State Militia. Inquiry into applicant's service in particular branch of United States Armed Forces.	Inquiry into an applicant's general military experience.
Organizations	Inquiry into the organizations of which an applicant is a member, excluding organizations of which the name or character indicates race, color, religion, national origin, or ancestry of its members.	Lists of clubs, societies, and lodges to which you belong.
References	Who suggested that you apply for a position here?	

References

1. Beilinson, J. "Workforce 2000: Already Here? Workforce 2000: Competing in a Seller's Market: Is Corporate America Prepared? *Personnel* 67(10):3, Oct. 1990.

2. *Effective Interviewing and Equal Employment Opportunity.* Philadelphia, Pa.: Haimes Associates Inc., 1989.

3. *Sexual Harassment Handbook for Managers and Supervisors.* Philadelphia, Pa.: Haimes Associates Inc., 1988.

4. *American Medical Association Policy Compendium* (1990 Annual Meeting Supplement). Chicago, Ill.: American Medical Association, 1990.

5. Little, B. "Why Can't a Woman be More Like a Man?" *New England Journal of Medicine* 323(15):1064, Oct. 11, 1990.

6. Kebanoff, M., and others. "Outcomes of Pregnancy in a National Sample of Resident Physicians." *New England Journal of Medicine* 323(15):1040-1045, Oct. 11, 1990.

7. Painter, J. *Maternity Leave Policies*, Report HH. Chicago, Ill.: American Medical Association Board of Trustees, 1990, pp. 1-90.

8. Painter, J. *Child Care in Hospitals*, Report J. Chicago, Ill.: American Medical Association Board of Trustees, 1990, pp. 1-90.

9. Thornburg, L. "On Site Child Care Works for Health Care Industry." *HR Magazine* 35(8):39-40, August 1990.

10. Knox, B., and Robinson, D. "Riverside Medical Center: Everyone's Satisfied (Child Care Benefits)." *Management Accounting* 71(10):30-1, April 1990.

11. Bichel, J. *Medicine and Parenting.* Washington, D.C.: Association of American Medical Colleges, 1991.

CHAPTER 7

WOMEN IN THE WORK FORCE: ISSUES FOR PHYSICIAN EXECUTIVES

by Rice Leach, MD, FACPE, and
Patricia D. Mail, MPH, CHES

*T*he increasing number of women in the work force is causing many changes in the character of the workplace, the rules under which it operates, and the behaviors that are conducive to a productive environment. As women exert their rights for a fair work environment and society supports them through new laws and personnel practices, management and male employees are finding it necessary to change their modus operandi rapidly. Styles, behaviors, and attitudes that were commonplace just a few years ago are no longer accepted and in many cases constitute cause for litigation. This chapter discusses some of the expectations women bring to the workplace, identifies changes in the laws and practices applicable to the workplace, and recommends behaviors that can assist managers and other employees deal with this steadily evolving environment.

INTRODUCTION

The last half of the Twentieth Century has seen women moving into the work force in increasing numbers, partly because families needed the additional income and partly because women wanted more job opportunities after filling many traditionally male jobs during World War II. The Women's Movement began, in the 1960s, to define and codify what women expected and demanded of society and of the workplace. A concerted cultural movement began in which women demanded access to industry, the professions, and nontraditional jobs that had been the exclusive domain of men.

Women believed that they should have access to all jobs and that they should receive equal pay for equal work. They were no longer willing to tolerate wage discrimination such as that recently reported in which male nurses earn 10 per cent more than female nurses.[1]

Women brought different expectations of how people should relate in work groups and how employees should be treated by one another and by management. They expected the same opportunities as men to be selected for jobs and to advance in careers. They wanted the same protection from safety and health hazards as men but also expected that the workplace would support their having children should they choose to do so. They expected to be able to work without being threatened or harassed by management or fellow workers.

At the same time women were identifying discriminatory practices in the workplace, the Civil Rights Movement and the population of older workers were identifying other forms of discrimination. The Civil Rights Act of 1964 and its subsequent amendments set the rules by which the United States defined and responded to discriminatory behavior. Furthermore, court rulings and personnel policy changes in the ensuing years have clarified and expanded definitions of behavior that constitutes discrimination.

As issues of equal opportunity, equal protection, and discrimination were evolving, management and employees were being forced to relinquish some previously appropriate activities and to learn new behaviors to enhance productivity and avoid complaints. Initial management responses to changes in the workplace were based on traditional male role models and caused tension when women's expectations were judged by criteria that had been appropriate for men but were not appropriate for women.

In the past 25 years, managers, personnel officers, consultants, and others have defined behaviors for organizations and individual employees to accommodate the requirements associated with an increasingly female work force and to avoid pitfalls associated with older behaviors.

WHAT DO WOMEN EXPECT?

About Equal Opportunity:

Women expect to have access to the increasing pool of job opportunities. They want to expand beyond the traditionally female jobs of teacher and nurse into traditionally male-dominated jobs such as fire fighter, chief executive officer, and cardiac surgeon. Women demanded (and continue to demand) equal pay for equal work and pay equity for comparable work.[2]

They expect to be able to enter the job market as competitive persons if their lives are disrupted as a result of dissolution of a marriage or for other reasons. Therefore, they expect that displaced homemakers will have support for and access to vocational and preprofessional training that will assist them in becoming self-sufficient.[3] They expect to see the end of stereotypes that can be discriminatory and hinder their career advancement. As an example, women must be mobile to get ahead, yet being mobile is perceived as "corporate disloyalty" in women but normal career progression in men. However, women indicate that they see no possibility of advancement through the "old boy network" in corporate settings and must take the initiative by seeking out more competitive positions with other companies. Current information supports these assessments by women. A recent survey of 110 male and female professionals from Fortune 500 companies in the Northeast found that 73 percent of the women quit their jobs to work for other companies where the opportunities were greater. Another 13 percent began their own businesses and 7 percent were seeking new jobs, again to increase their career opportunities.[4] Women constitute approximately 75 percent of the total health care labor force, and, in some categories, such as nursing and dental hygiene, the proportion is closer to 95 percent. Yet female administrators represent less than 15 percent of the affiliates of the American College of Healthcare Executives,[5] and only 5 percent of the membership of the American College of Physician Executives is female.[6]

Finally, women expect industry and government to change from long standing derogatory gender stereotypes and assumptions about women's place in society, women's health, and women's competency and competitiveness[7] to more current concepts that ensure equal opportunity for advancement in the corporate structure by acknowledging women's strengths, knowledge, and contributions.[8]

About Job Health and Safety:

Women expect to be given the same protection in the workplace as men,[9] and they want the protection without discrimination. Discriminatory practices are more likely in work settings where the majority of the workers are women or where men and women are treated differently for conditions that put both at risk. More women than men are likely to suffer repetitive strain injury associated with operating machines in certain low-status, low-pay jobs and are more likely to be exposed to the unknown risk associated with electromagnetic radiation from cathode-ray tubes used by data entry personnel because more women do the work than men.[10-12] To avoid liability, employers refuse to employ women in certain high-risk areas because they might become pregnant later and file claims. The women are denied the opportunity to earn the higher wages associated with the work. Women say that denying them access to these jobs is discriminatory because the jobs are a risk to both women and men. They further allege that management excludes females because of possible damage to a fetus rather than addressing the larger occupational safety and health issue and removing the risk to all employees.[13] In a specific example, women at the Johnson Controls plant in Milwaukee, Wisconsin, went to court to seek relief from a practice that excludes them from the battery production line because of a risk of lead exposure. They said that the lead exposure is a hazard to both sexes and that excluding them from the jobs on a basis of sex is discriminatory.[14] The United States Supreme Court found in favor of the women in March 1991 by declaring that "fetal protection" policies are a form of sex bias that is prohibited by federal law.[15] This conflict between fetal protection and equal employment opportunity for women has implications for health care organizations where women may be exposed to gas, radiation, and chemical risks or where women are not hired into such jobs to protect future children.

Women expect to be able to work without fear of being assaulted by other employees.[11] Today, women in low-status jobs are more likely to be assaulted. There is currently little protection against physical assault on the job, and neither women nor men are eligible for compensatory time or punitive damages when assaulted by fellow workers. The problem has been acknowledged and was included in the 1990 amendments to the Civil Rights Bill. These amendments were vetoed but have been reintroduced in the 102nd Congress.[11]

About Choosing Whether or Not to Have a Child:

Young women today expect to be able to work and to have choices related to marriage and childbearing.[16] Those who decide to raise families want pregnancy to be seen as a natural process and expect to be able to become pregnant and care for newborns without detrimental effects on their careers. They expect organizations to set aside previous stereotypes about working mothers and acknowledge that many women already return to the workplace after having children and that others would if adequate child care support existed.

Women have known for decades that if they chose to be mothers, their upward mobility was blocked on the assumption that they would quit to raise families. This attitude prevented women from being considered for promotion, advanced training, and career opportunities. Accordingly, many women chose the "career primary track" rather than the "mommy track" to remain competitive.[4] Many female executives who chose the career track and postponed pregnancy are now hurrying to have children before age becomes a contraindication.[17] Women workers who become pregnant report that they are viewed as abnormal because they do not follow the male professional role model[17] or as temporary employees because they cannot be "serious about their work."[12]

Available data suggest that these stereotypes about the pregnant working woman are unfounded, because most working women who take time out to have babies return to work within a year. Hughes reports that 50 percent are back in the work force by the time their children are three months old and 72 percent return by the time their children are one year of age.[17] Union leaders, in an effort to meet the needs of their female members, have identified the health needs of the mother and the child as significant issues in labor negotiations.[18] Women report difficulty obtaining proper child care because of inadequate numbers of qualified child care workers, inadequate child care worker salaries, nonexistent fringe benefits, and lack of adequate and uniform standards.[12,19] Adequate child care facilities would presumably result in still more women returning to the work force after having babies.

Finally, women expect the work environment to allow them to meet family needs and still be effective and creative on the job.

About Freedom From Sexual Harassment:

Women expect to be able to work without experiencing sexual harassment and they want sexual harassment against women to be defined according to women's expectations. Women have made it clear that they want a work environment where they do not have to tolerate giving sexual favors in return for employment benefits, do not have to tolerate touching or advances, and do not have to tolerate language, music, or graphic material that is sexually suggestive. The current prevalence of sexual harassment in the United States is confirmed by a survey of 36,000 federal employees by the Merit Systems Protection Board. Sexual harassment within the previous 24 months was reported by more than 40 percent of the women and by 15 percent of the men surveyed in 1980 and 1987.[20]

THE CHANGING LEGAL ENVIRONMENT

As the composition of the work force has changed and controversies have arisen, the legal and regulatory environment has become more supportive of women's demands.

Regarding Discrimination:

The Civil Rights Act of 1964 and its amendments[21] have caused the most change in the workplace by making discrimination and harassment illegal. The legislation lists specific prohibitions about discrimination on the basis of gender, including sexual harassment.

Equal Employment: Title VII, Section 703, of the Civil Rights Act as amended defines several employment practices as unlawful if done on the basis of race, color, religion, sex, or national origin. Specific discriminatory actions include failure to hire, compensate, promote, or discharge an employee; limiting or classifying employees or candidates; failing to refer for consideration; or failing to consider for training opportunities.

Harassment: The civil rights amendments defined sexual harassment as (1) explicit or implicit promise of career advancement in return for sexual favors; (2) explicit or implicit threats that the victim's career will be adversely affected if the sexual demands are rejected; and (3) deliberate, repeated, unsolicited verbal comments, gestures, or physical actions of a sexual nature.[21] These definitions have been further clarified and expanded by numerous court cases, and supervisors have been prosecuted and penalized by the Merit System Protection Board. Such prosecution reinforces the awareness that off-color joking, offensive physical contact, and other forms of harassment are no longer tolerated.[22] Recently, a federal judge addressed the issue of harassment and the "hostile environment" by ruling in favor of a female shipyard worker who found a display of lewd calendars and posters offensive. Judge Howell Melton ruled that women working in largely male environments are a captive audience for pornography and that pin-ups of nude women may well be offensive to the "average woman." The definition of hostile environment included not only nude pin-ups but was extended to include inappropriate verbal comments.[23]

Regarding Job Retention, Health, and Safety:

In 1990, legislation was passed that provided support to assist women in gaining initial entry to the work force. In recognition of discrimination against women who became pregnant, the 1978 Pregnancy Discrimination Act was passed to ensure that pregnant women are not required to leave the work force.[24,25] Nevertheless, even with some legal protection, women are still estimated to have lost over $31 billion annually in total earnings because of pregnancy-related job loss.[26]

The Congressional Caucus for Women's Issues has emerged as a major advocate for women. Founded by female members of Congress in 1977, the Caucus has focused primarily on economic concerns, such as pay equity, family leave, dependent care, pension reform, child support enforcement, and educational equity. More recently, the Caucus has begun to focus on issues of women's health and has specifically addressed breast cancer, osteoporosis, and teenage pregnancy.[3]

Recognizing the importance of economic issues for women, the Congressional Caucus for Women's Issues helped to secure passage of nine provisions to the Economic Equity Act during the 101st Congress. These provisions became amendments to various federal laws. Some of the major provisions of this omnibus legislation include[3]:

Vocational Education—requires funds to be set aside for programs designed to eliminate sex-role stereotyping in education and to provide opportunities for single parents and homemakers in vocational education.

Displaced Homemakers Home Ownership Assistance—supports displaced homemakers who have previously been part-owners of houses to participate in first-time home buyer programs.

Transitional Housing Child Care Services—provides funds for child care service programs for residents of transitional housing.

Domestic Violence—expresses the sense of the Congress that credible evidence of physical abuse of a spouse should create a statutory presumption that it is detrimental for the child to be placed in the custody of the abusive parent.

Public Housing Perinatal Services—authorizes 10 demonstration programs to create prenatal care facilities in public housing.

In addition to securing passage of laws to protect and extend services for women, the Caucus continues to track issues of major importance to women and provides appropriate regulatory and statutory support for matters of child care, family and medical leave, and women's health.

As evidence of the growing interest in women's health issues, the Public Health Service (PHS) elevated its Committee on Women's Health to the status of a full office in January 1991. As an Office of the Assistant Secretary for Health, it has the authority to coordinate interagency activities pertaining to women's health, including developing policy and monitoring implementation activities. Special foci will include attention to provider-patient communication between genders, cultures, and socioeconomic classes.[27] The Department of Defense has also established a formal mechanism to address the concerns of women through creation of the Defense Advisory Committee on Women in the Services (DACOW-ITS).

WHAT CAN MANAGERS DO TO HELP: RECOMMENDATIONS

Health care managers can effect a positive workplace for all employees and avoid difficulties by acknowledging that the environment has changed and that previously tolerated behavior is often no longer acceptable and by taking proactive steps to initiate organizational change. While health care organizations have many similarities with other organizations, they also have some unique characteristics that bring male and female providers into close and intimate contact and create settings for potential adverse actions against management. The credible performance of all actors in clinical situations is a key to avoiding potentially harassing situations.[28]

Acknowledging Change

It is clear that the traditional workplace has undergone major changes. These changes in the labor force and in the expectations of its newer members present new challenges to managers. They also present new opportunities. Managers need to acknowledge that female work styles differ from male work styles by being more participatory, more involving of others, and more sharing. Specific behaviors associated with this style include encouraging participation, sharing power and information, enhancing the self-worth of others, and energizing others.[29]

The successful manager will behave accordingly and will also minimize behaviors that reduce participation and sharing when working with female associates. Organizations that meet women on their own terms are more likely to attract, recruit, retain, and promote valuable female associates.

Monitoring Supervisory Behavior

Monitoring supervisory behavior to ensure fair treatment of all employees can stimulate the organization to address women's expectations and to avoid problems. Encouraging the organization to create opportunities for women to mentor other women helps. Holding managers accountable for how they assist in the career development of women and minorities under their supervision also has produced positive results.[4] A similar accountability measure has been suggested as a way to evaluate how well a supervisor or manager complies with Equal Employment Opportunity Commission requirements and company affirmative action policies. Members of the staff of the Public Health Service Federal Women's Program suggest that managers who continually select only one sex, in this case males, when the applicant pool contains qualified females should be counseled and corrective action taken if appropriate.[30] In some situations, such hiring patterns indicate underlying prejudice and hostility toward women. Managers are advised to address these situations before other behaviors result in complaints and grievances.

Evaluating Policies and Procedures

Evaluating personnel procedures and policies can avoid problems later on. In the health care setting, the chief executive officer, the medical director, and others should evaluate each step of the employment process to ascertain where and why women are having difficulty advancing within the organization. Comparing the organization's stated policies and procedures with actual practice is another way to identify opportunities for change. Cooper and Davidson[31] identify six "risk areas" of personnel policy that management must review to see that they don't encourage discrimination: job descriptions and personnel policies, recruitment and advertising, selection and appointment, promotion and lateral transfer, training and staff development, and conditions of service.

Avoidance of Stereotyping

Men and women need to work cooperatively to abolish the inappropriate sexual stereotypes that handicap both sexes' ability to explore their full potential. As Epstein notes in her response to Rosener,[29] "Women ought to be in management [or medicine] because they are intelligent, adaptable, practical, and efficient--and because they are capable of compassion."[32] The fact that opportunities for female physicians are still heavily concentrated in jobs caring for low-income patients, serving in underserved areas in the inner city, holding fewer academic appointments, less apt to be asked to serve on professional committees, and working fewer hours per week with fewer patients attests to the existence of opportunities to achieve a more equitable distribution.[33]

These sex and role stereotypes have developed over the years, but there are still actions that managers can take to minimize them. Rizzo and Mendez[7] suggest three ways to minimize gender stereotyping: Do not generalize about people, throw out stereotypes, and recognize that different situations will require different behaviors. Tension is also reduced when employees at all levels are encouraged to ask themselves[20]:

- Does my behavior contribute to work output and/or mission accomplishment?

- Could my behavior offend or hurt other members of the work group subjected to it?

- Could my behavior be misinterpreted, intentionally harmful, or harassing?

- Could my behavior send signals that invite harassing behavior on the part of others?

The recommended rule of thumb used in federal personnel training to avoid sex discrimination is "when in doubt, don't!" Joking and kidding about gender, race, age, and sexual orientation are inadvisable and can lead to complaints when there is a power difference by way of rank or position between two individuals or when there is a numerical imbalance between an individual employee and a group.[20]

SUMMARY

The manager in a health care setting must be aware of women's expectations at work, must realize that the legal and personnel environment has changed, and must behave accordingly to maximize the contributions of women in the work force and to avoid complaints and other adverse actions. Medical care settings have unique opportunities for positive change, such as improved provider-client communications,[34-36] improved research and service delivery,[37,38] and improved health for women and children and older women.[39,40] There are, however, accompanying risks in health care settings because of the intimate working relationships necessary to get the job done and because of the physical risks associated with health care settings. Management must make equal opportunity part of the corporate culture.

Rice C. Leach, MD, FACPE, is Chief of Staff, Office of the Surgeon General, U.S. Public Health Service, and Patricia D. Mail, MPH, CHES, is Chief, Professional Education, Alcohol, Drug Abuse, and Mental Health Administration, U.S. Public Health Service, Washington, D.C.

The assistance of the following individuals in the preparation of this chapter is deeply appreciated: Ann Ambler, Alcohol, Drug Abuse, and Mental Health Administration, Office of Equal Employment Opportunity and Civil Rights, Rockville, Md.; Agnes Donahue, Executive Director, Office of the PHS Coordinating Committee on Women's Health, Office of the Assistant Secretary of Health; Fran Buchanan, Director of Civil and Human Rights, Service Employees International Union, Washington, D.C.; Joan Farrar, Federal Women's Program Coordinator, Office of the Assistant Secretary for Health, U.S. Public Health Service, Rockville, Md.; Nora Howley, Research Assistant, University of Maryland, College Park, Md.; Kim Lessow, Congressional Caucus for Women's Issues, Washington, D.C.; Martin Levy, Policy and Program Coordination, Office for Equal Health Opportunity, Office of the Assistant Secretary for Health, U.S. Public Health Service, Rockville, Md.; Barbara Otto, Director of Program and Public Affairs, 9 to 5, Cleveland, Ohio; Carolyn Sparks, President, The Feminist Institute, Bethesda, Md.; Sim Tan, MD, FACPE, The Travelers Companies, San Diego, Calif.; and the Institute for Women's Policy Research, Washington, D.C. The opinions expressed in this chapter are those of the authors and do not necessarily represent the policy or the position of the U.S. Public Health Service.

References

1. *Women: The Road Ahead.* New York, N.Y.: Time, Inc., 1990.

2. *Bargaining for Pay Equity: A Strategy Manual.* Washington, D.C.: National Committee on Pay Equity, 1990.

3. Congressional Caucus for Women's Issues *Fact Sheet.* Washington, D.C.: Congressional Caucus for Women's Issues, 1990.

4. Trost, C. "Women Managers Quit Not for Family but to Advance Their Corporate Climb." *Wall Street Journal,* May 2, 1990.

5. Haddock, C., and Aries, N. Career Development of Women in Health Care Administration: A Preliminary Consideration." *Health Care Management Review* 14(3):33-40, Summer 1989.

6. *1991 Membership Registry.* Tampa, Fla..: American College of Physician Executives, 1991.

7. Rizzo, A., and Mendez, C. *The Integration of Women in Management.* New York City, N.Y.: Quorum Books, 1990.

8. Steinberg, R. "Social Construction of Skill, Gender, Power, and Comparable Worth." *Work and Occupations* 17(4):449-82, 1990.

9. "Protecting Women or All Workers?" *Women's Occupational Health Resource Center News* 1(3):1,6, 1979.

10. New U.S. "Guidelines on Reproductive Hazards." *Women's Occupational Health Resource Center News* 2(1):1,4, 1980.

11. Otto, B. (1991). Personal communication. Cleveland, Ohio: 9 to 5, National Association of Working Women.

12. Sweeney, J., and Nussbaum, K. *Solutions for the New Work Force.* Washington, D.C.: Seven Locks Press, 1989.

13. Mauer, M., and Weinbaum, P. "Reproductive Hazards in the Workplace—A Threat to Women, or All Workers?" *Labor Update* August 1981, pp. 9,14.

14. Bertin, J., and Ellis, D. *Memorandum on UAW vs. Johnson Controls.* New York, N.Y.: American Civil Liberties Union, Women's Rights Project, 1988.

15. Wermeil, S. "Justices Bar 'Fetal Protection' Policies." *Wall Street Journal,* March 21, 1991, p. B-1.

16. Olson, J., and others. "Having It All? Combining Work and Family in a Male and a Female Profession." *Sex Roles* 23(9/10):515-33, Sept.-Oct. 1990.

17. Hughes, K. "Pregnant Professionals Face Pressures as Work Attitudes toward Them Shift." *Wall Street Journal* Feb. 6, 1991, pp. B1, B5.

18. York, C. "The Labor Movement's Role in Parental Leave and Child Care." Washington, D.C.: Service Employees International Union, 1989.

19. Hartmann, H., and Pearce, D. *High Skill and Low Pay: The Economics of Child Care Work.* Washington, D.C.: Institute for Women's Policy Research, 1989.

20. Federal Women's Program. *Sex Discrimination Training Course.* Rockville, Md.: Office of the Assistant Secretary for Health, U.S. Public Health Service, 1990.

21. United States Code. The Civil Rights Act of 1964 as Amended. In *Title 42, The Public Health and Welfare* (Subchapter VI, Equal Employment Opportunities). St. Paul, Minn.: West Publishing Co., 1981.

22. *Donnell L. Jordan v. United States Postal Service.* Merit Systems Promotion Reporter, 44 MSPR 225, 1990.

23. Tifft, S. "A Setback for Pinups at Work." *Time* 137(5):61, Feb. 4, 1991.

24. Hughes, K. "Mothers-to-Be Sue, Charging Discrimination." *Wall Street Journal* Feb. 6, 1991, pp. B1, B4.

25. Women's Occupational Health Resource Center. *Fact Sheet—The Pregnancy Discrimination Act.* New York, N.Y.: Columbia University, School of Public Health.

26. Spaiter-Ross, R., and Hartmann, H. *Unnecessary Losses: Costs to Americans of the Lack of Family and Medical Leave.* Washington, D.C.: Institute for Women's Policy Research, 1990.

27. Donahue, A. Personal communication, Executive Director, Office of the PHS Coordinating Committee on Women's Health in the Office of the Assistant Secretary of Health, Feb. 7, 1991.

28. Emerson, J.P. "Behavior in Private Places: Sustaining Definitions of Reality in Gynecological Examinations." In Dreitzel, H. (Ed.), *Recent Sociology No. 2*, New York, N.Y.: Macmillan, 1970, pp. 74-97.

29. Rosener, J. "Ways Women Lead." *Harvard Business Review* 68(6):119-25, Nov.-Dec. 1990.

30. Farrar, J. Personal communication, Federal Women's Program Manager, Office of the Assistant Secretary for Health, U.S. Public Health Service, Rockville, Md., Feb. 6, 1991.

31. Cooper, C., and Davidson, M. "Preparing a Positive Action Programme." In *Women in Management.* London, England: Heinemann, 1985.

32. Epstein, C. "Ways Men and Women Lead." *Harvard Business Review* 69(1):150-1, Jan.-Feb. 1991.

33. Hojat, M., and others. "Differences in Professional Activities, Perceptions of Professional Problems, and Practice Patterns between Men and Women Graduates of Jefferson Medical College." *Academic Medicine* 65(12):755-61, Dec. 1990.

34. Lowe, M. "Women and Their Health Care Providers: A Matter of Communication— Introductory Remarks." In the *Proceedings of the National Conference on Women's Health*, Supplement to the July/August 1987 issue of Public Health Reports, p. 140.

35. Rogers, P. "Improving Communication between Women and Health Care Providers." In the *Proceedings of the National Conference on Women's Health*, Supplement to the July/August 1987 issue of Public Health Reports, pp. 141-2.

36. Ross-Lee, B. "The Physician-Patient Relationship." In the *Proceedings of the National Conference on Women's Health*, Supplement to the July/August 1987 issue of Public Health Reports, pp. 142-4.

37. Howes, J., and Bass, M. *Women's Health Research: Prescription for Change.* Washington, D.C.: Society for the Advancement of Women's Health Research, 1991.

38. Young, F. "Welcoming Remarks." In the *Proceedings of the National Conference on Women's Health*, Supplement to the July/August 1987 issue of Public Health Reports, pp. 1-3.

39. Barry, P. "Appropriate Health Care for Older Women." In the *Proceedings of the National Conference on Women's Health*, Supplement to the July/August 1987 issue of Public Health Reports, pp. 71-3).

40. Burst, V. "Issues and Concerns of Healthy Pregnant Women." In the *Proceedings of the National Conference on Women's Health*, Supplement to the July/August 1987 issue of Public Health Reports, pp. 57-61.

CHAPTER 8

GENDER AND VALUE ISSUES IN ORGANIZATIONS: CREATING THE ENVIRONMENT

by Susan L. Radecky, MD

*I*n this chapter, we will explore issues of gender and its relationship to cultural values of organizations, a topic that has not been the main focus of interest in the health care field. However, with diverse cultural values and the rise of gender issues, these factors will play an increasingly important role in organizational operations. Physician executives can more effectively serve their organizations if they provide leadership in this arena.

The author's assumptions are presented below so readers may better understand the context of the theories that will be addressed.

- Health care organizations have unique corporate cultures that represent the organization's values.

- Organizations vary in their awareness or emphasis on these cultural issues.

- The physician leader is responsible for creating an environment that will allow the organization to thrive.

- The most successful health care organizations of the future will be value- and gender-aware.

- Individual professionals vary in their gender- or value-awareness.

- Professional decisions are often value-based.

- As described in Maslow's concept of human needs, all people seek to achieve higher and higher levels of fulfillment as basic needs are realized.

SOME DEFINITIONS

A brief discussion of the definitions of "sex," "gender," "values," and the concept of "value-based decision making" will clarify the language of this chapter. "Sex" is that biologic description that can be categorized as female or male. "Gender" is a systems concept that functions as a social phenomenon of cultural categorization. The words "feminine" and "masculine" are gender system concepts. Because of this, traits or characteristics that are feminine or masculine cannot be easily categorized, because categorization of the traits is culturally dependent. It is helpful to understand this social systems phenomenon so that disputes regarding gender definitions can be brought into perspective.

The concept of "value-based decision making" draws on classical problem-solving schemes in which multiple options are generated after the problem is defined. After options are generated, selection of the best alternative leads to problem solution. The concept of "value-based decision making" asserts that selection of the best alternative often depends on an individual's or organization's values. Organizational values determine solutions that drive structural models to further support those values; this creates a dynamic triangular relationship of values-structure-actions.

THE ENVIRONMENTAL ASSESSMENT

Given these assumptions and definitions, the physician executive must first assess his or her personal and professional environment. An assessment will allow the physician executive to determine the existence of multiple cultures and values, identify areas of culture and value conflict, and develop a strategic plan for creating the desired environment.

Information generated from the assessment is designed to complement existing demographic and organizational information. The assessment tool described at the end of this chapter is an interactive model in which the physician executive meets with key organization people to assess dominant cultural values and gender awareness. In parallel, the physician executive meets with individual physician employees to assess their value and gender awareness. Finally, the physician executive must complete a self-assessment in order to evaluate his or her value and gender awareness.

Once this information is obtained, the physician executive will integrate the information so that gender and value issues can be effectively negotiated. First, the physician executive will create a description of the organizational climate. Second, having described cultures and values, the physician executive will identify areas of possible conflict between organizational leadership and employees. Third, having identified potential conflicts, the physician executive will develop options to resolve areas of conflict. In this process, there is active attention paid to clarifying issues, teaching both organizational leaders and employees, active participation in reframing issues, and facilitation of a win-win negotiating process. All of this occurs within the context of understanding how the physician executive's own biases will affect the process.

It is our observation that organizations and individuals vary greatly in their awareness of these issues, even though their behaviors are strongly influenced by the issues. A physician executive who is able to facilitate a productive discussion of value and gender issues will succeed in creating an environment that allows the organization and its professionals to achieve personal and professional satisfaction. At the same time, the personal and professional satisfaction of the physician executive will be enhanced as he or she serves as vision and voice in the health care system.

RATIONALE FOR ASSESSMENT OF ORGANIZATIONAL AND INDIVIDUAL VALUE AND GENDER AWARENESS

In order to expand the reader's understanding of the importance of assessing organizational and individual awareness of value and gender issues, three implications of avoiding the issue are presented. First, increasing diversity in physicians' values will create significant tension and distress within the organization. Second, organizational structure that has existed to control problems of diversity will result in organizations that are not able to function in a collaborative and innovative mode. Third, unresolved conflict within an organization can lead to paralysis.

Continuing changes in the health care environment will create significant tension in individuals within organizations. How this tension manifests itself will depend on the individual and on the organizational culture. Increased diversity in physician values will be an additional organizational tension if it is not managed in a constructive manner. One could assert that value diversity of professionals could become an easy target on which more global issues of distress will be projected. "Junior associates" are vulnerable in the organization and may fall prey to accusations related to values and gender; organizational leadership could be deceived in dealing with a problem that is a cultural rather than a personnel issue. A leader's success in assessing and managing the cultural issues of individual physicians within the organizational culture will determine his or her ability to create a positive environment.

Second, we assert a perspective of physician leadership that is creative and proactive. In this model, the physician leader's essential task is the creation of an environment that will allow the accomplishment of the organization's mission within the organization's structure. Leadership becomes an active, creative task of vision and voice.

Organizations that are dominated by physicians can become riddled with conflict--the result of turf battles, ego struggles, intellectual disagreements, etc. Unfortunately, organizational environments have heretofore frequently directly or indirectly fostered such conflict. In an attempt to manage a group of individualistic physicians, hierarchical and tightly controlled systems are devised. These systems are effective in determining the formal structure but are ineffective in changing behavior in the informal or corporate culture. An organization that allows the individual professional to collaborate, to maximize his or her individual efforts, to contribute to the organization without regard to rank within the system will help create an environment of innovation. This environment will also foster greater flexibility in resolving areas of value and cultural conflict.

Third, if a physician leader fails to deal with conflict, the organization can be paralyzed. The progression of issues may be from dissension among physician employees to increased tension within the organization overall, which leads to heightened stress among physician leaders and managers. As stress mounts, the ability and willingness of individual physicians to function productively may decrease. However, as the organization seeks to relieve organizational stress by recruiting additional physicians, the problem intensifies. The recruitment of a new associate becomes a fitting stage upon which to play all the mini-dramas of individual and corporate conflict. A perceptive potential associate will determine that this environment is not one that is suitable for personal and professional growth. A tradition of successful recruitment succumbs to an inability to recruit; unfortunately, the organization may never know why the recruitment process failed. If it is not aware of its own value and cultural issues, it can easily blame the recruitees instead of reflecting on the process.

These issues are examples of the cost of nonawareness. The assessment tool in this chapter is a model of how one would approach measurement of awareness. It should not be viewed as an evaluation tool. It is offered to individuals committed to exploring the gender and value sensitivity of their organizations and of their physician employees. Of primary importance is the ability of physician leaders to become more insightful so that they are able to create an environment conducive to personal and professional growth of all staff.

ASSESSMENT TOOLS

The following assessment tool is interactive and helps the interviewer appraise the gender and value awareness of the interviewee. Its format is based on the scientific model of inquiry. That is, the interviewer is actively involved in the generation of hypotheses, in the generation of questions to test those hypotheses, in the interpretation of data, and in the integration of this information. The interactive nature of the tool is essential, as the information we seek to measure includes significant subjective components. An assessment tool that concentrated only on a simple demographic analysis would not capture the gender and value awareness of the interviewees.

The interviewer seeks to make an assessment regarding the present status of these values in the organization or individual and to formulate a hypothesis regarding their future status.

Subsets of information have been listed beneath each category in the tools. These subsets are representative issues that will help the interviewer in the generation of hypotheses. Beneath the subset headings are examples of questions that will allow the interviewer to obtain information, test hypotheses, revise initial impressions, and confirm assessments. This format can be modified as the interviewer becomes more comfortable with and knowledgeable of the technique.

This assessment tool is of necessity subjective in nature. It has been developed in order to verbalize and thus make overt issues that have been predominantly subconscious or unidentified. Although it is labeled as an assessment tool, it should be used as a dynamic model. As the interviewer becomes more skilled in value determination and clarification, the tool will evolve. The ultimate purpose of the tool is facilitation of personal and professional growth in an organization.

Susan L. Radecky, MD, is Director, Grand Rapids Family Practice Residency, Family Care, P.C., Grand Rapids, Michigan.

I. ASSESSMENT TOOL FOR ORGANIZATIONS

GENDER AWARENESS

Demographics

How many women and men are in the organization?

What is the distribution of women and men in the leadership of the organization?

What is the medical specialty distribution of women in the organization? In the community?

Policy Development

Does the organization have a maternity policy?

Does the organization have a paternity policy?

What child care benefits are offered to employees?

Gender Safety—Gender Respect

What is your sense of how men and women interact within your organization?

How does the culture respond to a person on maternity/paternity leave?

Can you think of organizational activities that exclude people because of their gender? Are these exclusions appropriate?

VALUE AWARENESS—LIFE-STYLE

Physician Scheduling

Does the organization offer part-time or shared-time positions?

How much variability is there within the organization for physicians' schedules?

What barriers exist within your organization for an individual interested in a part-time, nontraditional schedule format?

After-Hours Call Scheduling

What is the organization's current call system?

What barriers exist within your organization for a physician who does not want to participate in after-hours work?

Personal Health—Professional Growth

What are the current benefits for vacation and meeting time?

What is the organization's policy on leaves of absence? Sabbaticals?

How does the organization encourage the personal and professional growth of its physicians?

VALUE AWARENESS—FINANCIAL

Individual and Corporate Roles

How does the organization determine physicians' salaries and benefits?

How much variability is there within the organization in physicians' reimbursement? Are these variations based on individual factors or organizational factors?

What are the barriers that exist within the organization for the physician interested in increasing reimbursement?

What is the corporate policy on moonlighting? What was the motive behind this policy?

Physician Ownership

What is the organization's interest in physician ownership? Is ownership desired or encouraged?

What is the motive for physician ownership? Financial? Control? Commitment?

What are the barriers that exist for a physician who is not interested in ownership?

II. ASSESSMENT TOOL FOR PHYSICIAN EMPLOYEES

CATEGORIES

- Gender Awareness

- Value Awareness—Lifestyle

- Value Awareness—Financial

GENDER AWARENESS

Demographics:

What has been your experience to date with the distribution of men and women in medical school? Specialty training? Professional experiences?

What are your interests regarding the number of men and women you would like to work with?

Describe an ideal physician associate.

Policy Developments

Is it important to you that your future organization have a maternity policy?

Is it important to you that your future organization have a paternity policy?

What role should an organization fulfill regarding child care?

Gender Safety-Gender Respect

What is your sense of how women and men should interact professionally?

Describe barriers that exist to effective interactions.

How will you respond when a professional associate chooses to go on leave? Because all people have gender biases, what gender bias do you have that may become problematic in future organizations?

VALUE AWARENESS—LIFESTYLE

Physician Scheduling

Is it important that an organization offer part-time and shared-time positions?

Do you anticipate the interest in defining nontraditional schedule formats for yourself?

How flexible should the organization be for its physician scheduling?

Describe the benefits and barriers that exist for a part-time physician associate.

After-Hours Call Scheduling

What call system would fit your needs?

How flexible should the organization be for physicians who do not wish to participate in after-hours call?

Personal Health—Professional Growth

What are your current interests regarding vacation and meeting benefits?

How flexible should the organization be for physicians who are interested in additional time away from the organization?

What is the organization's role regarding the personal and professsional health of its physicians?

Who is responsible for issues of physician impairment?

VALUE AWARENESS—FINANCIAL

Individual and Corporate Roles

How should a physician's salary and benefits be determined?

How much variability should exist within the organization in the salary structure? How responsible are you as an individual? What is the organization's responsibility regarding salary and reimbursement?

What is your perspective on moonlighting?

Given the significant level of indebtedness that new physicians are saddled with, what is an appropriate organizational response? How can issues of inequity be reconciled?

Physician Ownership

Is it important to you that you become an owner in your future organization?

What motivates you to become an owner? Financial? Control?

Describe how your position regarding ownership relates to your commitment to the organization.

III. SELF-ASSESSMENT TOOL

CATEGORIES

- Gender Awareness

- Value Awareness—Lifestyle

- Value Awareness—Financial

GENDER AWARENESS

Family of Origin

How does your family of origin deal with issues of gender? How much diversity/congruity is there with regard to female and male roles?

Are there significant events in your family that have contributed to your gender awareness?

How have your perspectives and biases regarding gender changed? What influenced those changes?

Gender Safety-Gender Respect

What is your sense of how women and men should interact professionally?

Describe barriers that exist to effective interactions.

Because all people have gender biases, what gender bias do you have that may become problematic for you?

Interrelationships

As you relate to others in your personal relationships, how divergent are your relations with women and with men? How similar is your significant other to the men or women you work with professionally?

How would you measure yourself regarding your sensitivity to gender issues? Think of an example that mirrors this judgment.

In the continuous cycle of human growth, where are you now in the life cycle? Where will you be in five years?

VALUE AWARENESS—LIFESTYLE

Personal Control

What are your biases regarding the issue of part time and shared time? What experiences created this bias?

Describe where you believe the locus of control should be between organization and employee.

How do your personal dreams regarding the way you would like to be influence your professional role?

Relationship to Physicians

What are your biases regarding the role of physicians in our society? Have your biases changed significantly in the past?

Drawing upon your total life experience, how responsive are physicians to discussions of gender and value?

Sketch the ideal physician associate and reflect upon the biases that create this image.

VALUE AWARENESS—FINANCIAL

Individual and Corporate Roles

What are your biases regarding the financial role of the individual within the corporation? The corporate to the individual?

Drawing upon your total life experience, how responsive are physicians to discussions of financial issues? How appropriate are their financial expectations?

Relationship to Physicians

What physician attributes create value for an organization? What bias does this reflect?

Describe how your own financial bias affects your professional relationship with physicians.

In your current stage of growth, how important are issues of finances and benefits? Has this varied over the past?

IV. ASSESSMENT TOOL—SUMMARY DOCUMENT

Given the information obtained through the interactive questions of the assessment tools for organizations and physician employees and the self-assessment tool intended for use by the physician executive or other change agent, the change agent should summarize the current gender and value awareness of the organization and of individual physicians. In addition, the change agent should predict future gender and value awareness of the organization and individuals. This summary is of necessity subjective in nature.

Organization's Gender Awareness

Present Status.

Future Trends.

Organization's Value Awareness—Lifestyle

Present Status.

Future Trends.

Organization's Value Awareness—Financial

Present Status.

Future Trends.

Physician's Gender Awareness

Present Status.

Future Trends.

Physician's Value Awareness—Lifestyle

Present Status.

Future Trends.

Physician's Value Awareness—Financial

Present Status.

Future Trends.

Organization's and Physician's Values—Areas of Congruence:

Organization's and Physician's Values—Areas of Divergence:

Organization's and Physician's—Strategies in Managing Areas of Convergence and Divergence:

EPILOGUE

by J. Sim Tan, MD, FACPE

*T*he gender-based themes discussed by various authors in this monograph reflect the attention employers are expending on their workers. During the past decade, American management literature has contained a growing number of books and articles attempting to provide answers for U.S. companies on human resource practices that would promote an integrated organization within the constructs of democratic ideals.

The economic realities the United States faces in health care services are no different from those facing companies in the financial and industrial sectors as well as government. We need to optimize and capitalize on our best resources, including our female labor pool.

All organizations are getting flatter, with whole layers of middle management being eliminated. Stockholders and investors, exerting pressure through boards of directors, are looking for the best qualified candidates to turn in top performances. The old charismatic leadership style is not enough. Instead, men and women who understand how to link employee compensation to productivity and performance, increase profits and decrease debt, and thoroughly execute a plan to reach these goals will be the new CEOs.

Successful companies of the future are in the process of revamping many of their strategies for human resources to encourage and speed integration of culturally diverse employees. Some basic assumptions that operate in the programs include:

- Endorsement of the worth of the individual, tailoring training to individual needs.

- Installment of reward systems commensurate with the culture and values of the organization, i.e., a caring culture that is also high on performance.

- Job enrichment programs to increase dedication and commitment and reduce turnover.

- Raising employees' trust level for the company so that creativity, innovation, and free speech are not punished (with time, activities that foster discussions of gender issues will expedite improved working relationships and productivity).

- Participation in decision-making, with opportunities for all employees to exercise their choices and become involved in implementation processes.

While some organizations cling to the past and refuse to recognize deficiencies in their approaches, change leaders are already embarked on employee-empowerment experiments as the first-step to building more cohesive teams. Physician executives can be among those change leaders.